REAGAN'S REIGN OF ERROR

There He Goes Again:
RONALD REAGAN'S REIGN OF ERROR

Mark Green &
Gail MacColl

with Robert Nelson
& Christopher Power

Design by
Charles Kreloff

Pantheon Books
New York

Copyright© 1983 by Gail MacColl,
Christopher Power, and The
Democracy Project, Inc.

Library of Congress Cataloging in
Publication Data
Main entry under title:
There he goes again.
   1. Reagan, Ronald—Quotations.
2. United States—Politics and
government—1981-
   I. Reagan, Ronald. II. Green,
Mark J.   III. MacColl, Gail,
E838.5.R437 1983   973.927′092′4
83-42812 ISBN O-394-72171-3 (pbk.)

All photos: UPI

Manufactured in the United States
of America

9876

To Mary Wentworth—G.M.

To my loving and Republican parents—M.G.

Authors' Note

The authors would like to give heartfelt thanks to those who so willingly contributed their time and expertise—without them this book simply would not have been possible. First and foremost, we thank our editor, Betsy Amster, whose guidance, patience, and enthusiasm we relied on throughout, and all others at Pantheon who were so gracious and helpful. We thank also: James Ainsworth; John Bickerman and the Center on Budget and Policy Priorities; Ron Brownstein and the Center for Study of Responsive Law; Mike Calabrese; Joan Claybrook; John Clewett and Critical Mass; Neal Cohen; Congress Watch; Tom Cosgrove and the National Clean Air Coalition; Steve Giardini; Greenpeace International; Betsy Houghteling and Joseph Houghteling; Robert McIntyre; Victor Navasky; Stan Norris at the Center for Defense Information; NYCLU; Martin Smith, Cecily Surace of the *Los Angeles Times;* Michael Waldman; and the staff of Wollman Library at Barnard College.

We owe a particular and separate acknowledgment to the many journalists who have been trying to differentiate Reagan fact from fiction for years—any mistakes herein are our own, but much of the credit is theirs.

Sources for quotes from Ronald Reagan are given in parentheses after each quote. "Radio" indicates that the quote was taken from transcripts of Mr. Reagan's nationally syndicated three-minute radio commentaries, which aired five times a week in the mid-seventies, except when he was an announced candidate for president. In the case of quotes from Reagan as President, the source, unless noted otherwise, is *The Weekly Compilation of Presidential Documents,* a publication of the National Archives and Records Service, G.S.A.

ABOUT THE AUTHORS

MARK GREEN worked for ten years with Ralph Nader, ultimately as head of his consumer lobby, Public Citizen's Congress Watch. The author or editor of eleven books, he is currently the president of The Democracy Project.

GAIL MACCOLL is a freelance writer and editor whose credits include *The Official Preppy Handbook* and *Items from Our Catalog.*

TABLE OF CONTENTS

THE BOTTOMLESS LINE

WANT ADS

AWFULLY LARGE OFFICES

UNKINDEST CUTS

KILLER TREES

SHORTAGE OF SENSE

THERE OUGHTA NOT BE A LAW

THE REST OF HIM

ADD YOUR OWN

"I will stand on, and continue to use, the figures I have used, because I believe they are correct. Now, I'm not going to deny that you don't now and then slip up on something; no one bats a thousand." (Philadelphia news conference, *Wash. Post,* 4/20/80)

INTRODUCTION:
The Great Communicator, or the Great Prevaricator?

— Mark Green

> **"** Politics is just like show business. You have a hell of an opening, coast for a while, and then have a hell of a close. **"** (Reagan to aide Stuart Spencer in 1966)

From young George Washington's apocryphal admission about chopping down a cherry tree to Jimmy Carter's political mantra in 1976 ("I will never lie to you"), the issue of presidential truth and consequences has long been with us. Since "example is leadership," to use Albert Schweitzer's phrase, Americans have expected—or at least hoped—that our leading citizen would be a truth teller.

Our 40th President, Ronald Reagan, appears sensitive to this expectation. "I've answered some questions with what I claimed were facts and figures. . . . But don't let me get away with it," he told a group of students in the White House on February 25, 1983. "If you have any questions as to whether any of my statements were not based on fact, check me out."

So we did. Gathering a quarter century of his remarks, we contrasted Reagan's assertions with authoritative sources. The process was factual, not ideological. That is, whether one is a conservative or liberal, loves or loathes him, it's important to know whether the President of the United States knows what he's talking about.

The resulting evidence irresistibly leads to one conclusion: No modern president has engaged in so consistent a pattern of misspeaking on such a wide range of subjects—and shown no sense of remorse. Prior presidents have committed their share of factual errors—and none of Reagan's approaches LBJ's deceptions about the war or Nixon's lies about Watergate. But in terms of sheer regularity and frequency, Ronald Reagan is the all-time champ. According to columnist James Reston, "I suppose more corrections have been put out of the White House on the public statements of Ronald Reagan than any other president I've known."

Reagan's problem is not merely the kind of innocent bloopers and *faux pas* all of us, even presidents, are prone to. Gerald Ford, for example, once actually said, "Things are more like they are now than they've ever been." Reagan, too, toasted Bolivia—in Brazil; referred to his Secretary of Housing as "Mr. Mayor" at a conference of mayors; called Samuel Doe, Head of State of Liberia, "Chairman Moe"; and announced at a GOP fund-raising dinner in 1982, "Now we are trying to get unemployment to go up, and I think we're going to succeed." No great harm done here.

Rather, this book brims with six kinds of errors that are far more serious than *faux pas*—obvious exaggerations, material omissions, contrived anecdotes, voodoo statistics, denials of unpleasant facts, and flat untruths. Let's consider each.

Reagan repeatedly exaggerates—or, to use Huck Finn's word, he tells "stretchers." There's often a kernel of truth here, but not much more. Yes, taxes as a percentage of GNP certainly rose from 1960 to 1981 (kernel), but they didn't *double* as Reagan exaggerated (10.4% to 12% are the accurate numbers). And yes, Pope John Paul mentioned Poland in a letter to Reagan following the crackdown on Solidarity, but the Vatican denied that the Pontiff approved of retaliatory US sanctions against Moscow, as Reagan's "stretcher" claimed. In each instance, the truth would not have been enough to sustain his point.

Reagan brings to mind Franz Kafka's remark about Martin Buber: "No matter what he says, something is missing." He

After several senators in a private meeting heard Reagan respond to questions about record budget deficits with a story of someone buying vodka with food stamps, Sen. Robert Packwood (R-Ore.) got fed up. "He's on a different track," he said about the President, adding that when he answers serious policy questions anecdotally, "We just shake our heads." (Associated Press, 3/1/82)

displays an irresistible impulse for what lawyers call a "material omission." At a March 1982 press conference, for example, he said the poor wouldn't suffer from his budget cuts because the federal budget was increasing by $32 billion; what he didn't say was that *all* of the increase and then some was for military spending, not social spending for the poor. The President repeatedly chides the food stamp program for increasing "16,000%," yet he is comparing the initial experimental program in a few counties to the final nationwide version.

Another misleading device is the use of apocryphal or unrepresentative anecdotes—or "anecdotage," in William Safire's coinage. Here we have battalions of welfare queens, students investing loan monies in money market funds, rich children getting free school lunches. Are these telling stories, or is Reagan telling stories?

Similarly, President Reagan often engages in what could be called voodoo statistics. When he wants to *inflate* a number, say the growth of federal spending, he'll always use absolute numbers not discounted for inflation ("In the last ten years, federal spending has increased more than 300%."). But when he wants to *minimize* a number, he'll either discount it for inflation (military spending will increase a "real" 10%) or give it in percentage terms (his budget deficit is "only" 5% of GNP).

Another form of error is the denial of fact. In a scene in Mel Brooks's film *Young Frankenstein*, Frankenstein meets his assistant Igor and expresses sympathy about the huge hump on his back. Replies Igor with a straight face, "What hump?" When it comes to stonewalling adversity, Reagan is Igor. After the 1982 mid-term elections, Reagan pronounced himself satisfied: "There was nothing to suggest a need to change the basic course." Nothing? How about the largest mid-term loss in the House (26) for a new president in a quarter century? And when scandal rocked the EPA in early

1983, he said the problem was merely unfair press reports; within three weeks, 13 top officials at the agency had resigned or been forced out.

Finally, there is the *summum malum* of misstatements—flat untruths. No kernel of truth here. President Reagan, for example, has said that the US decreased military spending in real terms over the past decade; that Brezhnev was the first person to propose the nuclear freeze; that John Hinckley bought his gun in a jurisdiction with a strict gun registration law; that we have as much forest area today as 200 years ago; that his administration hasn't "touched Social Security"; and that the federal education budget hasn't been cut. None of these statements is true.

D o all these examples mean that Ronald Reagan is a liar? No. Using Augustine's definition of lying as having one thing in your heart and another in your head, Reagan is telling the truth—not *our* truth, but *his* truth. He'd pass a polygraph test because, in a triumph of belief over reality, he seems to have persuaded himself that all his contrived anecdotes and funny numbers are accurate.

Is Reagan, then, reckless or negligent with the truth? Here, with sincerity not a defense, one can make a strong case. Exhibit One is the unblinkable volume of some 300 errors documented in this book—a volume that creates a strong presumption that the President either should have known his facts were wrong (negligent) or didn't care (reckless). Exhibit Two is his recidivism—errors repeated even after they are pointed out to him (e.g., claims that he vastly reduced the welfare rolls in California and that he has appointed more women to government posts than his predecessor). Exhibit Three is the way he uncritically passes along as fact information he gathers up as a vacuum cleaner lifts lint. When assistant David R. Gergen was quizzed about the source of Reagan's

NEWS ITEM°

"George Bush asserted today that there was 'a factual gap' in much of Ronald Reagan's campaign pitch. 'I think there's a factual gap, and I have to home in on it.' " (*New York Times,* 4/12/80)

NEWS ITEM

"There is a generation gap between what Reagan thinks he knows about the world and the reality," says John Sears, who ran Reagan's 1976 presidential campaign and half of his 1980 race. **"Reagan has all these old phonograph records in his head and a lot of them are full of misinformation. We used to talk about getting into his 'record library' and throwing some of them out."** (Interview, 4/28/83)

assertion that children were getting free school lunches in a community with an average income of $75,000, Gergen replied, "He heard it at a dinner party." Exhibit Four is how all his errors coincidentally lampoon big government and Democrats—and laud conservative Republicans and himself. Is there a method to his badness?

To next question has to be, *why* does Reagan err? Though motives are often mixed and murky, president-watchers need to try to decipher them in order to spur better presidential performance—or at least expose the most glaring lapses.

* *Ideology before evidence.* Reagan instinctively shoehorns all information to fit his ideological mold. Stories that demean welfare recipients are presumptively true and data that criticize the Pentagon are not to be trusted. So when presented with a situation that challenges his conservative catechism, like an unyielding Marxist-Leninist, he will change not his mind but the facts. And since his catechism about supply-side economics, civil rights, wealth and poverty, and the environment often clash with reality, Reagan is constantly engaged in circle-squaring exercises. Hence error.

* *Out-of-date/Out-of-touch.* His Norman Rockwell view of America—there didn't appear to be racial discrimination when he was a boy (sic); there weren't riots during the Great Depression (sic); local volunteer groups should have "barn raisers" to raise funds lost to budget cuts (sic)—is both appealing and absurd. It often appears that he made up his mind on most matters three decades ago and has been on automatic pilot ever since—a conclusion supported by identical phrasing in speeches decades apart. Reagan has a good memory for bad details.

* *Habit-forming.* Consider Reagan's careers before politics: acting, sportscasting, and lecturing. An actor succeeds or fails based not on the truth of what he says but the effect of lines scripted for him by others. "So much of our profession

is taken up with pretending," wrote Reagan in his autobiography, *Where's the Rest of Me?*, "that an actor must spend at least half his waking hours in a fantasy." As a sportscaster, Reagan, like all sportscasters of his day, would read wire copy and then make up colorful play-by-play commentary. Similarly, as a speaker for GE and conservative causes in the '50s and '60s, he developed the skill of delivering, and mentally cataloging for retrieval, punchy conservative shibboleths.

This background seems to have created a habit of mind that favors packaging over content, applause lines over accuracy.

* *Intellectual laziness.* This is different from the facile charge that he's "just a dumb actor." He was smart enough to get elected president and then get most of his economic program enacted. Yet family, friends, and aides will tell you that Reagan often substitutes personal charm and a sharp memory for the kind of hard work needed to master a topic. Here's Neil Reagan on his brother as a young man: "He would take a book the night before the test and in about a quick hour he would thumb through it and photograph those pages and write a good test. He uses the same method now when he speaks." Reagan himself told a biographer, "I'm a lazy fellow. I work up to a certain point, but beyond that point, I say the hell with it." He's long been famous for a 9-to-5 schedule with Wednesday afternoons off for riding—and he has taken more vacation time away from the White House than any president in decades. A *Newsweek* article in September 1982 quoted an unnamed White House aide as saying, "He probably spends two or three hours a day on real work." Perhaps as a result, delegations of members of Congress often leave closed meetings with him amazed at how uninformed he was on the subject discussed.

* *Isolation.* Reagan has long been isolated, rarely if ever exposing himself to a range of opinion that might dig him out

" It was easier if you weren't at the ball park because you didn't feel you were lying. What at the ball park might be just a blooper grounder to the shortstop—'and he digs it up, over to first base for an easy out'—could be different in a radio speech. Well, you didn't want to lose your audience, so you could say: 'It's a hard ground ball down toward second base. Jurges is going after the ball, makes a one-hand stab, almost falls down, gets him by half a step at first base.' I submit to you that I told the truth. . . . The truth got there, and, in other words, it can be attractively packaged. "
(*New York Times*, 6/27/76)

NEWS ITEM

"There are some uncomfortable moments, especially with guys like Trudeau, who have complete mastery of their dossiers and can talk about these things off the top of their heads. The President's not there yet, and my guess is that he won't ever be." (Presidential aide quoted in *Newsweek,* 9/7/81)

of his entrenched views. His insulated world of self-made businessmen and California conservatives reinforced his views that the Soviets and big government were behind everything. "When he asserts at a press conference that there were once two separate nations, one North and one South Vietnam, he's getting our facts wrong, not his," writes Nicholas Von Hoffman. "In the social and political circles he's lived in for the last three decades, there were two nations, one of which invaded the other. It is a fact."

His schedule for the past couple of years—whom he's met with and whom he's addressed—reveals a chief executive unfamiliar with America's diversity. In a three-week period in February–March 1983, for example, he addressed the American Legion, the National Association of Manufacturers, the National Association of Evangelicals, the Conservative Political Action Conference, and *The National Review*—groups that span America all the way from A to B. Indeed, Reagan is able to repeat the same one-liners, anecdotes, and errors in speech after speech, year after year, because he addresses only audiences that mirror his views.

The amiability factor. Finally, there's President Pangloss's upbeat and sunny personality. (Pangloss, the always optimistic tutor in Voltaire's *Candide,* would reiterate, despite a series of calamities, that all would turn out well and that this was the best of all possible worlds.) "You have to be careful with him," cautions a former aide. "If you had nine bad items to tell him and one good one, he would latch on to the tenth favorable item and discount the other nine." An upbeat personality is a nice trait in a friend, but can result in self-delusion when routinely applied to policy by a president. Acting sunny in a thunderstorm is charming, but you still get wet. And saying that budget cuts haven't hurt the poor or that tax cuts will increase tax revenues doesn't make it so. Writes Norman Miller, the Washington bureau chief of the *Wall Street Journal,*

"Frustrated Republicans say Mr. Reagan greets proposals for policy changes with silence, Irish jokes, or irrelevant pronouncements that he is glad that everyone agrees on fundamentals."

President Reagan and his aides dismiss the criticism that he is error prone. David Gergen, the head of communications at the White House, considers the issue trivial, a non-problem, "pure journalistic fantasy." "I don't think we ought to turn our presidents into statistical walking almanacs," he has said. "If you're a tenth of a point or two off on some number, that's not what's critical."

But denying an accuracy problem that has publicly bedeviled him since his 1966 race for governor simply compounds the problem. If there's no problem, why was top aide Stuart Spencer assigned to Reagan's campaign plane in 1980 to keep him from further gaffes? Why all the retractions coming out of the White House? Nor are all or most of the errors trivial. To believe that a Trident missile is recallable is hardly an insignificant blooper.

Condoning small mistakes in pursuit of a "larger truth" reveals the kind of casualness that tolerates and perpetuates error. "To lose faith in his attestations on small things," writes columnist Murray Kempton of the President, "means all too soon to distrust them in large ones." In fact, the evidence for Reagan's "larger truths" is pretty thin as well. For example, he campaigned prominently against a "window of vulnerability" on nuclear arms and "Democratic deficits" that cause inflation. The President now has implicitly accepted the premise of the bi-partisan Scowcroft Commission that there was no "window of vulnerability." As for deficits *causing* inflation, Reagan's are unprecedented, yet inflation is down.

Taking a different approach, Rep. Richard Cheney (R-Wyo.), who was President Gerald Ford's chief of staff, said in an interview that President Reagan's misstatements were "no worse than those of other presidents."

True, all presidents feel the pressure to throw a coat of bright varnish on everything they touch. Sometimes that has included engaging in misrepresentations, stretchers, untruths—even deceptions and lies. Ike allowed his State Department to say a U-2 downed in Russia was just a stray weather plane. The White House said that JFK cancelled a political trip in October 1962 due to a cold when the real reason was the discovery of Soviet offensive missiles in Cuba. LBJ deceived the public on the costs of the Vietnam War and on the Tonkin Gulf resolution.

Richard Nixon's cover-up of Watergate, of course, is the quintessential example of presidential deception. As for Jimmy Carter, he often grossly exaggerated when talking about himself as a candidate in 1976; for example, he was not a "nuclear physicist." But critics and supporters interviewed for this introduction agreed that, when President, Carter made very few errors of fact when discussing policy.

Rep. Cheney, then, is correct in implying that Reagan is not the first erring president, but wrong in concluding that he's no worse than his predecessors. Could someone fill a book this long with Carter's factual failures? Ford's? Ike's or JFK's? Even Nixon's or LBJ's? The answer appears to be no, though dissenters are welcome to try. One might contend that Reagan is different merely in degree, but this many degrees is the difference between hot and cold running water.

Despite this record, President Reagan shows no sign of contrition or concern; one high Reagan aide has said, "I have never heard him say, 'I was wrong.' " Eisenhower quickly acknowledged the truth about the U-2. JFK assumed full responsibility for the Bay of Pigs. "But with a *chutzpah* unprecedented in the theater of politics," concludes Professor Richard Phelps of Indiana University, who has studied Reagan's use of statistics, "Reagan spews out false facts with nary a pause or flinch. He shows no shame."

Perhaps it is because Reagan has essentially gotten off easy in the media for his misstatements. To be sure, there was a flurry of press reports about them early in the 1980 presidential campaign and then early in 1982. Though the errors didn't subside, the press reports did. (Some journalists diligently continue to report them, like Lou Cannon of the *Washington Post*, but such stories have slipped further and further back from page one.) As for the electronic media, journalist Robert Kaiser observes that "the television networks have a hard time reacting. They haven't found a formula for saying the President is wrong." So 30 million people hear President Reagan's well-delivered speech, and 10 reporters and op-ed rebutters later pen pieces correcting him. The result: he's way ahead in audience and credibility. A false remark gets halfway around the world, remarked Mark Twain, before truth puts on its boots.

Shaking his head in dismay, Rep. Mo Udall (D-Ariz.), in an interview, said that Reagan "has an immunity, as if he's not judged in the same courtroom." Why? Because of the triumph of charm over content. Reagan is a near-genius at deflecting charges about misstatements with an array of deft jokes, rhetorical questions, changes of subject, shoulder shrugs, sheer reiteration ("I was right on five of them . . ."), and personal indignation (". . . every fiber in my being opposes racial discrimination"). So his trained sincerity on television is credible even if his material isn't. In the opinion of John Sears, "If Jimmy Carter were making these mistakes, he would be treated much worse. The press didn't like Carter on the level of a personal human being. But they like Reagan, and this affects their intensity factor."

President Carter found this out the hard way. Rick Hertzberg, who was Carter's speechwriter, recalled how

« For many years now, you and I have been shushed like children and told there are no simple answers to the complex problems which are beyond our comprehension. Well, the truth is, there are simple answers. »

(Inaugural message, 1/5/67)

Reagan made so many obviously false assertions in the climactic 1980 campaign debate—e.g., he never favored voluntary Social Security, he never expressed indifference to nuclear proliferation—that "Carter didn't bother correcting him, assuming the press would crucify him. But they didn't." Indeed, when Reagan taunted Carter with his now legendary line, "There you go again," he was factually wrong: Carter had said Reagan opposed Medicare in 1965, which was true. Carter won the debating point, but lost the audience and the election.

The pattern and frequency of Reagan's untruths create significant public costs, Gergen's attempted trivializations notwithstanding.

First, there's the effect on officials in his administration, who may understandably consider it standard operating procedure to make misleading remarks to advance their purpose. Vice-President George Bush actually denied he ever criticized candidate Reagan for his "voodoo economics." (He did, on tape, at Carnegie-Mellon University on April 10, 1980.) OMB Director David Stockman effectively admitted he doctored economic indicators to make administration projections look good in 1981.

Second, there's the effect of Reagan's disinformation on the content of public policy. In the popular acronym of computer programmers, it's GIGO (garbage in, garbage out). When he says convincingly that President Coolidge's tax cuts resulted in increased tax revenues (they didn't), it may have converted a close vote on his tax bill into an easy win. And when he says repeatedly that the Soviets dominate us militarily (no member of the Joint Chiefs of Staff has ever believed this), it has to help enact his record-setting military budget. Here distortion is not harmless but pivotal.

The final cost of false facts is a loss of trust in government. Every presidential untruth, when unmasked, makes it harder for subsequent presidential information to be accepted and acted on. So when, in mid-1983, Reagan urges the public to trust his assertion that he doesn't intend to send troops to fight in Central America, he may be telling the truth—but how can we be sure, given his documented penchant for false statements? Sissela Bok, in her book *Lying: Moral Choices in Public and Private Life,* put the problem well:

> *Imagine a society, no matter how ideal in other respects, where word and gesture could never be counted upon. Questions asked, answers given, information exchanged—all would be worthless. A warning that a well was poisoned or a plea for help in an accident would come to be ignored unless independent confirmation could be found. . . . Trust is a social good just as much as the air we breathe or the water we drink.*

Whatever the short-run gains by dissembling and feinting, the best rule—for incumbents and all their heirs—is that you can't lead people by misleading them. Unfortunately, Ronald Reagan, as Abraham Lincoln once said of an opponent, appears to have such a high regard for the truth that he uses it sparingly. "Ignorance is preferable to error," remarked Thomas Jefferson, "and he is less remote from the truth who believes nothing, then he who believes what is wrong."

NEWS ITEM

In response to a question by reporter Bruce Drake at a February 1982 press conference, Reagan said, "You don't really want to get into those mistakes you said that I made the last time, do you?" Warming to the subject and waving a bunch of papers, the President added, "I'd like you to know that the documentation proves that the score was five to one in my favor. I was right on five of them and I have the documentation with me." When reporters later asked White House aides to disclose the "documentation," they refused. (2/18/82)

REAGAN GAFFE EARLY WARNING SYSTEM

Don't sit defenseless during news conferences, hoping against hope that he's got it right. Be able to tell when Ronald Reagan has just dropped a big one. Protect yourself and your family from all magnitude of incoming error. The Reagan Gaffe Early Warning System (R.G.E.W.S.) is an easy-to-use defensive weapon designed to withstand exaggeration and distortion launched by our 40th president, up to and including obscure federal budget calculations. Constructed of the most durable substance known to man—reason—R.G.E.W.S. is completely hardened to statistical blur, off-the-cuff anecdote, avuncular charm, and diverting rhetoric. *Installation is completely free.*

1. COMMON SENSE GAP. Exercise your skepticism. Please. If you find yourself saying, "Gee, that sounds funny to me," perk up—you're probably right. Reagan's potent biases lead to distortions that even a moderate amount of good sense can combat. Keep your own intuitive alarm system in good working order.

2. THE AUTHORITATIVE SOURCE. Any Reagan assertion that has sweep and authority is suspect. Such assertions often open with statements like, *"As history shows . . ."* or *"As a recent study/report/investigation shows. . . ."* Misleading information generally follows. A variation on this approach is the UNFAMILIAR QUOTATION: *"As FDR/JFK/Winston Churchill once said. . . ."* (They didn't.)

3. THE CASE HISTORY. The storyteller in Reagan loves to cite individual histories to explain general policy. The sentence will usually begin, *"I recently heard of a man who. . . ."* Case histories have a tendency to turn into TALL TALES.

4. THE CLINCHING DETAIL. Reagan relishes percentages, numbers with decimal points, statistics, dates. It all sounds so concrete. Would a president say 77.3% if it weren't correct? This one does, all the time.

5. THE FALSE FACT. *"For instance"* and *"as an example"* are Red Alerts—any information following these phrases must be questioned. The example given is likely to be a double threat—both wrong and unrepresentative. Reagan likes to universalize the aberrant—don't let him.

6. DENIAL. When you hear Reagan say at a news conference, *"Well, that just isn't so,"* in a tone of patient dismay, you can bet it *is* so.

7. REITERATION. *"As I have said many times . . . "* is one of Reagan's favorite verbal tags. Most of the time he really has said whatever he's about to say many times, in which case it has, through repetition, become hardened in error. But then again he may never have said it before in his life.

8. RHETORICAL QUESTIONS. When deserted by both fact and anecdote, Reagan will ask a rhetorical question. This question will pivot on what debators call "the planted axiom," a premise that is assumed to be true but is never actually discussed or defended.

9. THE DEMOCRATS. Reagan has been a standardbearer for the far right a lot longer than he's been a leader of all the people. Any time he explains his policy in terms of the mistakes the other party has made, be on the alert for major historical revisionism.

10. THE BIG WRAP-UP. In a conclusive and pre-emptive tone, Reagan often polishes off his argument with a definitive statement — a FUN FACT, perhaps—and it sounds like a cogent and biting summation of the issue. It's not.

THEY'RE ALL DIFFERENT COUNTRIES
Reagan & Foreign Policy

Ronald Reagan has never been much of an international globe-trotter. He has trouble remembering the names of other nations' leaders. He has only the sketchiest notion of other nations' histories. He likes to maintain a "Battle of the Super Powers" approach to foreign policy—that way he doesn't have to learn about other countries because they're only pawns in a larger struggle. Keep it simple, keep it clean. If a nation declares itself anti-Soviet it is, *de facto,* a "democracy." On the other hand, an insufficiently anti-Soviet foreign government is, *ipso facto,* "totalitarian" ("authoritarian" if it gets lucky and Jeane Kirkpatrick is feeling generous). There can be no end of praise for dictators in Argentina, in Korea, for Marcos in the Philippines and Pinochet in Chile—they are good men fighting the good fight. Human rights only complicate the issue. If Reagan could have it all his way, the world would be run as a high school color day: choose up sides, the blues against the reds; everybody has to play; only one side can win. Then we'd know how things stood, wouldn't we?

❝ *[Kissinger aide Sonnenfelt] has expressed the belief that in effect the captive nations [in Eastern Europe] should give up any claim of national sovereignty and simply become a part of the Soviet Union.* ❞ *(Time, 4/11/76)*

Time magazine's Washington correspondent Strobe Talbott reported that "nothing in any version of Sonnenfelt's remarks justified Reagan's charge."

WISHFUL THINKING DEPT. ➤

❝ *[The Canal Zone] is every bit as much American soil as is the land in the states that were carved out of the Gadsden and*

Louisiana purchases, as is the state of Alaska. **99** (*New Republic,* 4/17/76)

No, it's not. The Canal Zone was never US territory; its citizens were not automatically citizens of the US, as are the citizens of, say, Alaska. The US, in its 1903 treaty with Panama, was given the image of sovereignty, the right to behave as "if it were the sovereign," but never legal sovereignty. The US Supreme Court made reference to this in its *Vermilya-Brown Co. v. Connell* decision (1948): "Admittedly, Panama is territory over which we do not have sovereignty."

66 *Arriving in Warsaw in 1977 President Carter got off the plane to announce to a startled satrap who rules that country on behalf of the Soviet Union, 'Our concept of human rights is preserved in Poland.'* **99** (*Wash. Post,* 2/4/80)

A staple of Reagan's basic campaign speech. Simply put, Carter never said any such thing.

66 *There has been an attempt to harass those who are sympathetic with freeing Cuba.* **99** (*Wash. Post,* 3/10/80)

When pressed for specific cases of such harassment, Reagan stated that he had "no examples." As one reporter persisted, Reagan claimed, "I've got to keep moving," and left the room. His assertion left advisers as well as journalists nonplussed.

66 *I remember when Hitler was arming and had built himself up—no one has created quite the military that the Soviet Union has, but comparatively he was in that way. Franklin Delano Roosevelt made a speech in Chicago. . . . In that speech, he called on the free world to quarantine Nazi Germany, to stop all communication, all trade, all relations with them until they gave up that militaristic course and agreed to join with the free*

WHAT A DIFFERENCE A DAY MAKES

1/7/80:

"I just don't believe the farmer should be made to pay a special price for our diplomacy, and I'm opposed to [the Soviet grain embargo]." (*Wash. Post,* 1/8/80)

1/8/80:

"If we are going to do such a thing to the Soviet Union as a full grain embargo, which I support, first we have to be sure our own allies would join us on this." (*Claremont* [NH] *Eagle Times,* 1/9/80)

◄ UNFAMILIAR QUOTATION

In December 1982, after a meeting with Guatemalan military ruler General Efrain Rios Montt, President Reagan said that Montt was getting a "bum rap," and was "totally dedicated to democracy." But Montt (who proudly told the President, "We have no scorched earth policy—we have a policy of scorched Communists") had already announced in August 1982 a state of siege so the government could, he said, "kill people legally."

According to Amnesty International, Montt's government has practiced "widespread killing, including extrajudicial execution of large numbers of rural noncombatants, including entire families as well as persons suspected of sympathy with violent or nonviolent opposition groups."

nations of the world in a search for peace . . . but the funny thing was he was attacked . . . for having said such a thing. Can we honestly look back and say that World War II would have taken place if we had done what he wanted us to do back in 1938? **"** (3/3/81)

Try 1937. And can we honestly put words in FDR's mouth? Nowhere in FDR's "Quarantine Speech" did he refer to Hitler or Nazi Germany, nor did he appeal to the "free world" to isolate Germany. FDR was probably referring to imperial Japan, which had just renewed its attack on Nationalist China. Finally, FDR was not "attacked for having said such a thing"—the public response to the speech was largely favorable.

" *We think that we are helping the forces that are supporting human rights in El Salvador.* **"** (3/6/81)

Think again. Twelve thousand people were killed in El Salvador in 1980. According to Amnesty International, the "majority" of those murders were committed by the military, and it is the military regime that the US is "helping" in El Salvador.

" *Can we abandon this country [South Africa] that has stood beside us in every war we've ever fought?* **"** (*New Republic*, 5/2/81)

Perhaps the President would find abandonment of South Africa and its apartheid policies easier if he knew that the Afrikaners, South Africa's current ruling party, *opposed* South Africa's entry into both world wars but were overruled by the then-governing pro-British majority. In fact, every South African prime minister since 1948, except one, was imprisoned during World War II for pro-Nazi sympathies.

PROS & CONS:

The Olympic Boycott

66 *How can we condone putting the Olympics in Moscow? . . . I support the idea of taking the Olympics someplace else.* 99 (*Lansing* [MI] *Journal, 2/14/80*)

66 *I favored the boycott, but since we are going to be the only ones I find myself worrying about the young people who trained so long. I don't like withholding visas. Leave it to the athletes.* 99 (March 31, *New York Times, 4/6/80*)

The government was not withholding visas and did not threaten to do so.

66 *If just one country doesn't show up, I think the Soviet propaganda machine probably grinds out something like the United States didn't come because they were afraid of getting beaten.* 99 (*Wash. Post, 4/1/80*)

At least 25 other governments supported Carter's appeal for the boycott.

66 *We should boycott the Moscow Olympics. I think our allies should, too.* 99 (April 4, *New York Times, 4/6/80*)

66 *I just cannot within myself now find it right that the President of the United States should now be able to say to Americans who have violated no laws or anything, that they cannot go and cannot leave this country.* 99 (*New York Times, 4/9/80*)

The boycott was always voluntary—the United States Olympic Committee voted to support Carter's appeal and urged its athletes not to attend the Summer Games in Moscow.

66 *I support the boycott today, I supported it yesterday. And I supported it when the President first called for it.* 99 (*New York Times, 4/11/80*)

China Syndromes

I n mid-August 1980, George Bush was dispatched to the Far East to prove that Reagan had a coherent foreign policy for that part of the world. This arrival of the Republican team upon the international scene was less than entirely successful. In fact, Ronald Reagan's comments—such as referring to Taiwan as the "free Republic of China"— seemed designed to spoil his running mate's stay in Peking. (Source for all quotes: *The New York Times* August 20, 24, 25, 26, 1980.)

This "liaison" would violate the Taiwan Relations Act of 1979, ruling out official government relations between the US and Taiwan.

5/17

REAGAN:

"One of the things I look forward to most if I am successful in this election is to re-establish official relations between the United States government and Taiwan. . . . That liaison office [in Taiwan] is unofficial. It is not governmental. It is a private kind of thing. And I have said before that I see no reason why, with an embassy in Peking, we could not now have an official liaison office in Taiwan. . . ."

8/16

REAGAN:

Q: "Do you advocate a 'government to government relationship' with Taiwan?"

A: *"Yes, I think that liaison—this is what I stress—that could be official."*

8/16

BUSH:

"I will articulate as best I can the objectives of the Reagan foreign policy and they will be refreshingly received in Peking, I can assure you."

8/19

BUSH:

"Governor Reagan hasn't proposed a two-Chinas policy, nor does he intend to propose such a policy. We don't advocate diplomatic relations with Taiwan, nor have we."

8/22

REAGAN:

Q: *"Are you still for 'official relations' with Taiwan, yes or no?"*

A: *"Um, I guess it's a yes."*

8/23

PEKING:

"[Mr. Reagan's] remarks are absolutely not a slip of the tongue. He has insulted one billion Chinese people."

8/23

BUSH:

"No comment."

8/25

REAGAN:

"I don't know that I said that or not, ah, I really don't."

8/25

BUSH:

"He did not say that. If you're referring to the press conference I attended, the Governor did not say 'government to government relations.' "

8/25

REAGAN:

"I misstated."

NEWS ITEM

In an attempt to downgrade President Carter's initiative on US–China policy, President Reagan said, "In the first place, China relations had been normalized by the visits of a previous President to a previous administration [i.e., Richard Nixon]. And I am not at all sure that [Carter] added anything to what had already been accomplished." (*Wash. Post*, 5/5/83) Carter added, of course, what *Washington Post* columnist Philip Geyelin labeled "the hard part"—the 1979 "normalization" agreement that established full diplomatic relations between the two countries.

DEPT. OF RETRACTIONS

After Mr. Reagan said he stood behind a campaign statement that Jerusalem should remain united under Israeli sovereignty, the White House was forced to issue a clarification on American policy in order to head off an international misunderstanding.

Although confirming that he had been quoted correctly, the White House indicated that the President's statement was not an accurate expression of administration policy. That policy remains support for an undivided Jerusalem whose ultimate fate will be decided by negotiations on a peace plan for the region. (*New York Times*, 11/20/81)

❝ *I've had a lengthy communication from the Pope. He approves what we've done so far.* **❞** (1/19/82)

Reagan's communication from the Pope may have been lengthy, but as the Vatican hastened to point out, it did not involve approving Washington's sanctions against Moscow after the crackdown in Poland.

❝ *I said there was a flurry about land reform [in El Salvador]. I understand that that has turned around, that there are thousands of people who have been given deeds to their plots. . . .* **❞** (7/29/82)

As of January 1983, according to the administration's own figures, not even one thousand Salvadorans had been given final title to their land as a consequence of the government's land reform program.

❝ *We have never interfered in the internal government of a country and have no intention of doing so, never have had any thought of that kind.* **❞** (9/28/82)

Never? That's not what an article on the front page of the *New York Times* on December 4, 1982, said: "United States covert activities in Central America, which began a year ago with limited aims, have become the most ambitious paramilitary and political action operation mounted by the CIA in nearly a decade, according to intelligence officials." Nor is it what the President himself said half a year later: "Now, if they [House Committee members] want to tell us that we can give money and do the same things we've been doing—money giving, providing subsistence, and so forth to these people [anti-Sandinista guerrillas] and making it overt instead of covert—that's all right with me." (*Wash. Post,* 5/5/83)

❝ *Well, I am pleased to announce today that the industrialized democracies have this morning reached substantial agreement to a plan of action. The understanding we've reached demonstrates that the Western alliance is fundamentally united. . . .* **❞** (Radio speech, 11/13/82)

Had France and England suddenly been stricken from the list of industrialized democracies? After Reagan made this announcement lifting pipeline sanctions against the USSR, British Foreign Minister Pym said that the European governments had made "no concessions" in return for what he said had been "a unilateral decision by the Americans." And France flatly contradicted the President's statement, asserting that it was "not a party to the agreement announced this afternoon in Washington."

❝ *We are not trying to do anything to try and overthrow the Nicaraguan government.* **❞** (4/14/83)

Consistent with the Boland Amendment, which prohibits the US from trying to overthrow the Nicaraguan government, the President maintained throughout early 1983 that US aid to anti-Sandinista guerrillas who *are* trying to overthrow that government was only an effort to persuade Nicaragua to stop shipping arms to El Salvador. Then, in an interview with reporters in May, President Reagan four times characterized those anti-Sandinista guerrillas as "freedom fighters"—a term he has not yet used to designate guerrillas in El Salvador. According to *Newsweek,* "Red-faced White House staff men did their best to dampen speculation that Reagan had been deceitful—or simply disengaged—by stressing that he was speaking from the heart." Which, no doubt, he was.

❝ *Our purpose, in conformity with American and interna-*

NEWS ITEM

Speaking in June 1982 the President described Syrian missiles in Lebanon as "offensive weapons," adding, "There's no question about the direction in which they're aimed." Well, naturally, there is *some* question, since the weapons under discussion are surface-to-air missiles used for anti-aircraft purposes—they are, therefore, aimed in the direction of whatever is flying over them and are entirely *defensive* in nature. (*Wash. Post,* 6/17/82)

" I remember a happier time when there was a tradition that the President of the US never left our shores, but I don't say that you could do that today. "
(*Time*, 11/17/80)

A LESSON FROM HISTORY ➤

tional law, is to prevent the flow of arms to El Salvador, Honduras, Guatemala, and Costa Rica. " (4/27/83)

Such a purpose does not conform to law, at least not according to one hundred law professors from all over the United States who, in a statement last year, declared that the administration's plan to covertly destabilize the government of Nicaragua constituted a serious violation of both international and domestic law. They stated that the charter of the Organization of American States prohibits "covert destabilization of any O.A.S. member state." Article 15 of the charter provides: "No state or group of states has the right to intervene, directly or indirectly, for any reason whatever, in the internal or external affairs of any other state. The foregoing principle prohibits not only armed force but also any other form of interference or attempted threat against the personality of the state or against its political, economic, and cultural elements."

" If you remember, the Organization of American States asked Somoza to resign at that time. And Somoza, his reply to them was that if it would benefit his country, Nicaragua, he would. And he did resign. " (5/4/83)

Somoza did officially resign from office, but only under threat of his life. By July 17, 1979, the morning Somoza fled to Miami, the Sandinistas had already set up an interim government at Leon, Nicaragua; had surrounded Managua, the capital of Nicaragua, on all sides; and were rapidly closing in on the city. Possibly the next day, and no later than July 19, the Sandinistas occupied Managua and the National Guard disbanded. So Somoza "resigned," not because it would "benefit" his country, or because the OAS had asked him to do so eight months previously, but because he wanted to save himself. The man Somoza chose to succeed him as president lasted in office no more than 30 hours.

"But we are the ones who have gone a step beyond that [Camp David agreement] with regard to trying to have an overall peace in the entire area. That had never been proposed." (5/4/83)

According to columnist Philip Geyelin writing in the *Washington Post,* overall peace "has been proposed in the so-called Rogers plan under Nixon and regularly by Henry Kissinger; it is the bedrock of the Camp David Accords." Indeed, the preamble to the Accords states: "The parties are determined to reach a just, comprehensive, and durable settlement of the Middle East conflict."

"Well, I learned a lot. . . . I went down [to Latin America] to find out from them and [learn] their views. You'd be surprised. They're all individual countries." (Wash. Post, 12/6/82)

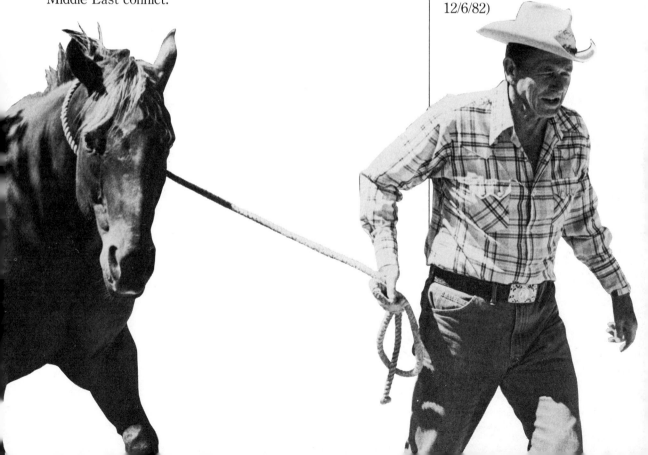

Vietnam, A Noble Cause

Maybe the reason Ronald Reagan thinks the Vietnam War was "a noble cause," thinks it was "a war which our government refused to win," thinks there is "no parallel between Vietnam and El Salvador," is that he really doesn't know much about it. Or, to put it another way, what he thinks he knows is mostly wrong. Two lengthy renditions of the History of the Vietnam War According to Ronald Reagan have been made available by their originator—in a January 1978 radio speech and a February 18, 1982 presidential press conference. Both are sadly garbled.

❝ *There were two Vietnams, north and south. They had been separate nations for centuries.* **❞** (Radio, Jan. 1978)

When not artificially divided by the Chinese or French colonialists, Vietnam was politically united for much of its history.

❝ *Both became colonial possessions of France in what was known as French Indo-China and both were freed a few years after World War II as one after another of the European colonial empires were liquidated.* **❞** (Radio, Jan. 1978)

Under French colonization, Vietnam was divided into three administrative units: Cochin China, Annam, and Tonkin. In 1950, these three sections were unified by the French under Emperor Bao Dai. The French did not "free" any part of Vietnam. It was taken from them by Vietnamese anti-colonial forces during a long and bitter conflict that culminated in the battle of Dien Bien Phu, where the French were handed a decisive loss. President Eisenhower turned down a French request for American bombing support at Dien Bien Phu, although by that time the US was bankrolling the French effort.

This battle took place in the spring of 1954, nearly a decade—not "a few years"—after WW II.

PROBLEM SOLVING

« We should declare war on North Vietnam . . . We could pave the whole country and put parking strips on it, and still be home by Christmas. » (Fresno Bee, 10/10/65)

« Vietnam returned to its pre-colonial status as two nations. The great powers in Geneva set down a plan, first, to allow the people of both countries to move to whichever of the two they chose without interference, and second, for an internationally supervised election by the people as to whether they wanted to unite or continue as separate nations. » (Radio, Jan. 1978)

The first sentence is meaningless, as Vietnam did not have pre-colonial status as two nations. As for the great powers in Geneva, the Geneva Conference of 1954 set up a *temporary* partition of Vietnam at the 17th parallel and called for *national* elections to be held two years later. The brand-new government of South Vietnam refused to sign the Geneva accords or to participate in elections, which were never held. The accords did not stipulate a ballot question on uniting or separating for the simple reason that they treated Vietnam as a single country, making no mention of two separate states. The US would not give even oral consent to the Final Declaration of Geneva, the part containing a call for free general elections.

« The Communist dictator of North Vietnam, Ho Chi Minh, refused to hold the elections and when a million of his people started moving south away from communism (under the terms of the agreement) his troops barricaded the frontier and halted the migration. » (Radio, Jan. 1978)

Once again, it was the newly created South, not the North, that refused to hold elections. In fact, Ho Chi Minh complained when balloting did not occur. President Eisenhower, in his memoirs, stated that experts agreed that "possibly 80% of

LITTLE KNOWN FUN FACT

"Because Vietnam was not a declared war, the veterans are not even eligible for the G.I. Bill of Rights with respect to education or anything." (*Newsweek*, 4/21/80)

Sure they are. Even if Vietnam wasn't a declared war. Apparently Reagan's mind wandered during an earlier meeting with two high-ranking military officers who were trying to tell him that peacetime veterans of the all-volunteer army did not receive education benefits.

SPECIAL REPORT #2

the population would have voted for the Communist Ho Chi Minh as their leader" if elections had been held. The armistice section of the Geneva accords provided a 300-day period of civilian movement across the demilitarized zone at the 17th parallel. During this period, the US Seventh Fleet helped some 860,000 people, mostly Catholics, move from the northern zone to the southern, where a devout Catholic named Diem was assuming control. Ho's troops didn't have to "barricade the frontier"—it was closed to civilian movement at the end of the 300-day period.

❝ *And openly, our country sent military advisers there to help a country which had been a colony have such things as a national security force, an army if you might say, or a military to defend itself. And they were doing this, I recall correctly, also in civilian clothes, no weapons, until they began being blown up where they lived in walking down the street by people riding by on bicycles and throwing pipe bombs at them, and then they were permitted to carry sidearms or wear uniforms. . . .* **❞** (2/18/82)

The United States Military Assistance Advisory Group, in uniforms, with weapons, arrived in South Vietnam in the late '50s to create and train a South Vietnamese army. By the early '60s, as insurgency grew and the troubled Diem regime crumbled, "combat support"—in the form of what was, by 1963, 16,000 American soldiers ("advisers")—was supplied to the army of the Republic of South Vietnam. To suggest that uniforms and weapons were withheld from American troops in Vietnam until they were being blown up by pipe bombs thrown from bicycles is ludicrous.

66 . . . *but . . . when these attacks and forays became so great, . . . John F. Kennedy authorized the sending in of a division of marines, and that was the first move toward combat moves in Vietnam.* **99** (2/18/82)

In the face of a rapidly deteriorating military and political situation—of somewhat larger proportions than "attacks and forays" on individual American soldiers—the first official American ground troops were sent to Vietnam. They were in the form of two—not one—US Marine Corps divisions, and they landed at the US air base in Danang in March 1965—nearly a year and a half after JFK's assassination.

66 *I have a feeling that we are doing better in the war than the people have been told.* **99** (*L.A. Times,* 10/16/67)

FOCUS OF EVIL
Reagan & the USSR

When it comes to the Red army, the President puts his voice-in-the-wilderness pedal to the floor: he repeats his warning—they're bigger than we are, they're better than we are—even if he must stand alone. And alone he has stood, as administration figures and even Republicans hesitate to join him in awarding the #1 superpower slot to the USSR. (According to the Department of Defense's own Annual Report for fiscal 1982, "The United States and the Soviet Union are roughly equal in strategic nuclear power.") America doesn't need all that much convincing on the subject of the Soviet menace, so why the hyperbole? Sure they've been pursuing a defense build-up program, sure they've got new weapons, sure there's cause for concern, but as the Reagan rhetoric heats up, skepticism may be the only way to keep cool. And an America skeptical about huge increases in defense spending is not what Ronald Reagan has in mind.

FALSE ALARM

❝ *Kissinger is quoted as saying that he thinks of the US as Athens and the Soviet Union as Sparta. [Kissinger says] 'the day of the US is past, and today is the day of the Soviet Union. . . . My job as Secretary of State is to negotiate the most acceptable second-best position available.'* **❞** (TV speech, *New York Times*, 4/1/76)

Reagan did not cite sources. Kissinger, denying the remarks, said that as an historian he could not have made the Sparta-Athens analogy because "Athens outlasted Sparta by several centuries." Lawrence S. Eagleburger, a State Department counselor, called the remarks "pure invention and totally irresponsible." James Reston pointed out that the accusation originated with Admiral Elmo R. Zumwalt, Chief of Naval Operations (1970–74). According to Reston, Zumwalt was quoted in *Parade* magazine, "which had the decency to publish a flat denial that Mr. Kissinger had said anything of the sort. Mr. Reagan was not so fair."

❝ *As a matter of fact, where this [report on USSR military capability] came from is the defense expert of the Library of Congress. . . . He said for a time it was our qualitative advantage that kept us ahead in spite of their quantitative advantage. But he had to say that no longer is true.* **❞** (*New Republic,* 6/12/76)

The report said that our qualitative advantage was less than it used to be, but that we still had it. See below.

❝ *Sen. Clark, of Iowa, [stated] that he asked the military experts of the Library of Congress to give him a report and admitted that he wanted it because he believed that all this talk and all of the administration requests for more money was because they were just simply building a scarecrow to get more money for defense. And so he thought he would get a report from the Library of Congress that would bear this out and he had to admit himself that he got a report from the Library that was probably more terrifying than any of the statements I have made— the report that we were indeed in a very dangerous position.* **❞** (*New Republic,* 6/12/76)

Reagan made these comments in an interview with John Osborne, who then discovered that it was Sen. John C. Culver, not Sen. Dick Clark, who asked for the report from the Library of Congress. According to Culver's defense specialist, the Senator and his staff did not expect the report to say any particular thing; they were not "surprised" by what they got; the report concluded that the margin of US superiority was smaller but still there; Sen. Culver never got close to characterizing the report as "terrifying."

❝ *Let us be aware that while they [the Soviets] preach the supremacy of the state, declare its omnipotence over individual man, and predict its eventual domination of all peoples of the earth— they are the focus of evil in the modern world.* **❞** (3/8/83)

FALSE ALARM

"On balance, the Soviet Union does have a definite margin of superiority [in nuclear arms]." (3/31/82)

"I don't think there'd be much accomplishment in freezing the Soviet Union into a position of superiority over the rest of us." (6/1/82)

"The Soviet Union does have a decided edge on us [in nuclear forces]." (7/11/82)

"Unless we demonstrate the will to rebuild our strength and restore the military balance, the Soviets, since they are so far ahead, have little incentive to negotiate with us." (11/22/82)

General David C. Jones, former chairman of the Joint Chiefs of Staff, said that he would not swap the American defense establishment for the Soviet one. According to former Secretary of State

❝ . . . *We are second in military strength to the Soviet Union. . . . The chief of engineering and research at the Pentagon, the top defense expert at the Library of Congress, the Secretary of the Army, and others have all stated and upheld this fact of where we are now in this second-best position.* ❞ (*New York Times,* 6/27/76)

Each of the gentlemen mentioned had, on occasion, pointed to limited areas of Soviet military advantage. But the Ford administration and the Department of Defense maintained that there were also significant areas of American advantage, adding up to a "rough equivalence" over all.

❝ *Up until now [the Soviet invasion of Afghanistan] the Soviet Union has not used its own military forces in its imperialism. It's taken over country after country, but it's done it with proxy troops.* ❞ (*Des Moines Register,* 1/8/80)

Soviet troops were used in Hungary in 1956 and in Czechoslovakia in 1968.

❝ *And so, in addition to their great military buildup, they [the Russians] have . . . practiced evacuation, when we finally began to learn the facts, we learned that in one summer alone, they took over 20 million young people out of the cities to the country to give them training in just living off the countryside.* ❞ (Robert Scheer interview, Feb. 1980)

We? Nobody but Reagan seems to know about the Soviet evacuation of young people—the CIA says that there is no evidence the Russians have ever practiced evacuating their cities.

❝ *Yes, they [the Russians] have gone very largely into a great civil defense program, providing shelters, some of their industry is underground and all of it hardened to the point of being able to withstand a nuclear blast.* **"** (Robert Scheer interview, Feb. 1980)

Scheer asserts in his book, *With Enough Shovels,* that he could find no expert who believed that all of Soviet industry is hardened to the point where it could withstand a nuclear blast. He also points out that the September 1978 CIA study of the Soviet civil defense program—the only complete CIA study of the subject—could find no evidence of hardened industry and that even those given to thinking the worst of the Russians could go no further than a belief that some industry is protected—and only against the indirect effects of a bomb.

" *Today, we are not equal to the Soviet Union, and that is why they were able to cross into Afghanistan.* **"** (*The New Yorker,* 3/24/80)

There must be other reasons—an unquestioned US military and nuclear superiority did not seem to deter Soviet troops from crossing into Hungary in 1956, or 12 years later into Czechoslovakia.

" *Now, the Soviets have 945 warheads aimed at targets in Europe in their medium-ranged missiles. And we have no deterrent whatsoever. . . .* **"** (10/14/82)

Hardly. The US now has, on submarines in both the Atlantic and the Mediterranean, 400 warheads targeted at the Soviet Union. Also on these subs are all additional 4,500 warheads not officially committed to NATO. Great Britain has 192 warheads targeted at the USSR; France has 98. The President is also ignoring the bomber forces of both the US and NATO, which have the capacity to drop well over 1,000 nuclear weapons on the USSR.

FALSE ALARM CONT.

Alexander Haig, "our systems are both more sophisticated and reliable and more technologically sound" than the Soviets. And Defense Secretary Caspar Weinberger reported to Congress that the US arms buildup was intended to "prevent the Soviet Union from *acquiring . . .* superiority"— not keeping it.

◄ **HUH???**

NEWS ITEM

In a November 1982 address to the nation, Reagan asserted, "Today, in virtually every measure of military power, the Soviet Union enjoys a decided edge." One month later, during an interview with Independent Radio Network correspondents, he was asked, "Would you trade American forces for Soviet forces?" His reply: "No."

PROBLEM SOLVING

❝ Why shouldn't the Western world quarantine the Soviet Union until they decide to behave as a civilized nation? ❞ (New York Times, 1/17/80)

❝ Soviet leaders invest 12–14% of their country's GNP in military spending, two to three times the level we invest. ❞ (11/22/82)

Misleading—our GNP is twice theirs. So the 6–7% of our GNP that we invest in military spending is roughly equal to their 12–14%. Besides, both the Pentagon and the CIA admit that they don't know how much the Soviets spend on defense. However, the Pentagon does estimate that in the past decade, according to the prestigious Institute for Strategic Studies, the US and its NATO allies outspent the USSR and its Warsaw Pact allies by $300 billion.

❝ The Soviet Union put to sea 60 new ballistic missile submarines in the last 15 years. Until last year we had not commissioned one in that same period. ❞ (11/22/82)

According to the *New York Times* (11/24/82), there is virtually unanimous expert judgment that American submarines, despite their age, remain decidedly superior in overall performance.

❝ The Soviet Union has built over 200 modern Backfire bombers—and is building 30 more a year. For 20 years, the US has deployed no new strategic bombers. ❞ (11/22/82)

Again, prevailing military judgment in the US Air Force is that the B-52, despite age, is a better long-range bomber than the Backfire.

❝ The Soviet Union has deployed a third more land-based intercontinental ballistic missiles than we have. Believe it or not, we froze our number in 1965 and have deployed no additional missiles since then. ❞ (11/22/82)

We don't believe it. While the *number* of missiles hasn't changed since 1967—not 1965—the *quality* has. Minute Man IIs and IIIs have replaced the original Is. In addition, every administration, beginning with Richard Nixon's, has chosen to increase the number of nuclear warheads on each missile, rather than the number of missiles, a choice experts say was deliberately made for strategic reasons.

❝ *This is what they [the Russians] said of themselves. That they reserved these rights to break a promise, to change their ways, to be dishonest, and so forth if it furthered the cause of socialism. Now, just the other day, one among you [journalists] somewhere has written and commented on that and has quoted the ten commandments of Nikolai Lenin . . . the ten principles—guiding principles of communism. And they're all there. That promises are like pie crusts, made to be broken. . . .* **❞** (1/20/83)

Lenin did make the pie crust reference, but he used it as a criticism of the conduct of his political opponents, not as a justification for his own actions. Discussing political infighting, Lenin wrote: "The promises, like pie crust, are leaven to be broken, says the English proverb." The search for the "Ten Commandments of Communism" continues.

❝ *Certainly their [the Soviet Union's] entire beliefs—beginning with the disbelief in God—their entire beliefs are so contrary to what we accept as morality. Witness a Kampuchea and an Afghanistan and so forth.* **❞** (3/18/83)

Morality and politics don't always mix. Witness the fact that it is the United States, not the Soviet Union, that recognizes Pol Pot's Khmer Rouge as the legitimate government of Kampuchea. It was under Pol Pot's reign, from 1975 to 1979, that an estimated three million Cambodians were massacred.

TEMPTATION OF PRIDE
Reagan & Defense/
Disarmament

More tanks. More bombers. More carriers and destroyers. Reagan wants so much more of everything that explodes that his own Republicans are getting jittery. Even John Connally and William Simon want him to slow down. As for arms control, the President never liked the idea of fewer nuclear weapons in the arsenal. After all, his opponents on the issue are dupes of Soviet propaganda. His source? *Reader's Digest,* probably (the FBI has been of no help at all). When you look at the buildup, never underestimate the power of Reagan's anti-Communist paranoia. Behind it all lies an absolute belief in Soviet military superiority. Haven't we heard this one before? Remember the bomber gap, the missile gap, and the ABM gap? The President does. And he's nostalgic for them, even though they never existed. Do you also remember the recent CIA discovery that the Soviets' real defense growth was not the 4% assumed but actually closer to 2%? You might as well forget it. The President already has.

UNFAMILIAR QUOTATION ▶

❝Secretary of State Kissinger has expressed the view that you and I, the American people, lack the will and the stamina to do what is necessary to keep this country #1.❞ (New York Times, 6/27/76)

Kissinger repeatedly disavowed any such statement. Reagan never backed it up with evidence, nor did he stop saying it.

❝I am not talking of scrapping. I am talking of taking the [SALT II] treaty back, and going back into negotiations.❞ (Presidential debate, 10/28/80)

Reagan had been virulently anti-SALT II for some time,

although he softened his position as the election approached. Some sample comments: "Send it back to the Soviets so fast they'll think we've got a new postal service"; "SALT II—ship that thing back to the Soviets in Moscow." Or from January 1980: "I've flatly called for shelving the SALT II treaty."

❝ *Besides which, it [SALT II] is illegal, because the law of the land, passed by Congress, says that we cannot accept a treaty in which we are not equal.* **❞** (Presidential debate, 10/28/80)

Whether or not the SALT II treaty was a good idea, it did not explicitly establish the US as being unequal to the USSR. Even if it had, it would still be legal if ratified by the US Senate.

❝ *We then went back into negotiations on their [the Soviets'] terms, because Mr. Carter had cancelled the B-1 bomber, delayed the MX, delayed the Trident submarine, delayed the Cruise missile, shut down the . . . Minute Man missile production line. . . .* **❞** (Presidential debate, 10/28/80)

The B-1 bomber had been delayed. As for the rest: the Cruise missile and MX were under full-scale development; the Minute Man missile's production line had been shut down because the production schedule had been met; and the first Trident submarine, the USS *Ohio*, had been launched on April 7, 1979.

❝ *. . . I would like to correct a misstatement of fact by the President. I have never made the statement [that nuclear proliferation is 'none of our business'] about nuclear proliferation, and nuclear proliferation, or the trying to halt it, would be a major part of a foreign policy of mine.* **❞** (Presidential debate, 10/28/80)

❝ *So in your discussions of the nuclear freeze proposals, I urge you to beware the temptation of pride—the temptation blithely to declare yourselves above it all and label both sides equally at fault, to ignore the facts of history and the aggressive impulses of an evil empire, to simply call the arms race a giant misunderstanding and thereby remove yourself from the struggle between right and wrong, good and evil.* **❞** (3/8/83)

◀ UNFAMILIAR QUOTATION

Q: "Do you think there could be a battlefield exchange without having buttons pressed all the way up the line?"

A: "Well, I would—if they realized that we—if we went back to that stalemate, only because our retaliatory power, our seconds, or our strike at them after their first strike would be so destructive that they couldn't afford it, that would hold them off." (10/17/81)

❝ We're in greater danger today than we were the day after Pearl Harbor. Our military is absolutely incapable of defending this country. ❞ (*New York Times,* 4/12/80)

Jacksonville, Florida, January 31, 1980: "I just don't think it's any of our business. All of us would like to see non-proliferation—but I don't think we are succeeding. We're the only ones in the world that's trying to stop it." (*New York Times,* 2/1/80)

❝ But I do believe this: that it is rather foolish to have unilaterally disarmed, you might say, as we did. . . . ❞ (3/3/81)

The United States did not disarm in the '70s; it dramatically strengthened its nuclear forces. Some of the programs: (1970–75) Replacement of Minute Man I and II ICBMs with 550 Minute Man IIIs; (1970–76) MIRVing of 550 Minute Man III ICBMs; (1971–76) Replacement of Polaris A3 SLBMs with 496 Poseidon C-3 SLBMs; (1971–76) Addition of 65 FB-111 SAC bombers and 356 F-111 nuclear-capable bombers; (1971–77) MIRVing of 496 SLBMs on Poseidons; (1972–75) Addition of 1,140 short-range attack missiles to B-52 and FB-111 bombers; (1979–83) Retrofitting of 900 MK12A warheads on 300 Minute Man IIIs; (1979–82) Retrofitting of 192 Trident I missiles on 12 Poseidon submarines; (1976) Initiation of Trident submarine program; (1981) Air-launched Cruise Missile operational; the first of at least 4,350 to go on B-52s; (1970s) B-52 and FB-111 improvements—20 programs; (1970s) ICBM improvements—5 programs. In 1970, the United States had 4,000 strategic nuclear warheads. By the end of the decade, it had almost 10,000.

❝ There is one area, however, where we must spend more and that is for our national defense. Now don't get me wrong. Cap Weinberger . . . has shown me programs in his department where we can and will realize substantial savings. We'll cut

$2.9 billion in next year's budget alone, and the cuts will accumulate to more than $28 billion by 1986 in the Defense Department. **99** (3/30/81)

Twenty-eight billion dollars over five years is approximately 2% of the defense budget—as compared to a nearly 100% increase in that proposed budget over the same period from $182.9 billion in 1982 to $377 billion in 1988.

66 *I do have to point out that everything that has been said and everything in their [Soviet defense] manuals indicates that, unlike us, the Soviet Union believes that a nuclear war is possible. And they believe it's winnable. . . .* **99** (10/17/81)

Not unlike us. The US Army field manual *Nuclear, Biological and Chemical Reconnaissance and Decontamination Operations* from February 1980 says, "The US Army must be prepared to fight and win when nuclear weapons are used." Senior adviser to the National Security Council (1981–82) Richard Pipes' views were summarized in the *Washington Post* as follows: "His strategy, which he says reflects official thinking, is a winnable nuclear war." And the US budget for Fiscal Year 1983 states, "US defense policies ensure our preparedness to respond to and, if necessary, successfully fight either conventional or nuclear war."

66 *During the last 10 years, the United States decreased its military spending.* **99** (1/14/82)

66 *As you can see . . . in constant dollars, our defense spending in the 1960s went up because of Vietnam. And then it went downward through much of the 1970s.* **99** (11/22/82)

Not so. According to the controller of the Department of Defense, the US defense budget, in 1982 constant dollars,

LITTLE KNOWN FUN FACT

66 *I recently learned something quite interesting about video games. Many young people have developed incredible hand, eye, and brain coordination in playing those games. The air force believes these kids will be our outstanding pilots should they fly our jets.* **99** (3/8/83)

❝ *I could see where you could have the exchange of tactical [nuclear] weapons against troops in the field without it bringing either one of the major powers to pushing the button.* **❞** (10/17/81)

WISHFUL THINKING DEPT. ➤

was *$179.9 billion* in 1971, while we were fighting a war with Vietnam; in 1981, that constant dollar figure was *$193.9* billion.

❝ *The leader of Ground Zero does not believe in the freeze. A freeze, yes, but after, as we've said so many times, a verifiable, substantial reduction to bring us down to parity and at a reduced number.* **❞** (4/20/82)

Roger Molander, the head of Ground Zero, said that "the President really misrepresents my position on the freeze." Though he has not taken a position on the freeze proposal, Molander disagrees with Reagan's view that the Soviet Union possesses nuclear superiority over the United States.

❝ *Those [nuclear weapons] that are carried in ships of one kind or another, or submersibles, you are dealing there with a conventional type of weapon or instrument, and those instruments can be intercepted. They can be recalled.* **❞** (5/13/82)

Submarine-launched missiles cannot be recalled. If the President thinks differently he may be surprised in a nuclear exchange.

❝ *What we're striving for is to reduce the power, the number, and particularly those destabilizing missiles that can be touched off by the push of a button.* **❞** (5/13/82)

The destabilizing impact of land-based ICBMs is not that they can be touched off by the push of a button. They can't be. They destabilize the balance between American and Soviet nuclear forces because their great accuracy might encourage a preemptive nuclear first strike. Nevertheless, this administration is going ahead with the two most accurate and destabilizing missiles ever built—MX and Trident II.

" *There is no question about foreign agents that were sent to help instigate and help create and keep such a movement [the nuclear freeze movement] going.* " (11/11/82)

Reagan's comments refer to the huge anti-nuclear rally—almost one million people—held in New York's Central Park on June 12, 1982. Edward J. O'Malley, assistant director of intelligence for the FBI, told the House Select Committee that fall that he "would not attribute the large turnout" to Soviet agents. Rep. Edward Boland, chairman of the committee, said his panel's hearings led to the conclusion that "Soviet agents have had no significant influence in the nuclear freeze movement."

" *Incidentally, the first man who proposed the nuclear freeze was in February 21st, 1981, in Moscow—Leonid Brezhnev.* " (12/10/82)

Nope. The freeze idea was first officially proposed by Sen. Mark Hatfield (R-Ore.), in 1979, as an amendment to SALT II.

" *You have to remember, we don't have the military industrial complex that we once had, when President Eisenhower spoke about it.* " (1/5/83)

What we do have is the military industrial complex Eisenhower was trying to warn us against. In that famous farewell address, Ike said, "We must guard against the acquisition of unwarranted influence . . . by the military industrial complex. The potential for the disastrous rise of misplaced power exists and will persist."

" *I was the one who took the lead to begin bringing about the first real arms reduction talks that we've ever been able to hold with the Soviet Union. . . .* " (2/16/83)

" *You start with the fact that the government has a sizable layer of fat, no matter how worthwhile the program. And I would include defense in that.* " (*Newsweek,* 3/24/75)

◄ LITTLE KNOWN FUN FACT

◄ UNFAMILIAR QUOTATION

◄ WISHFUL THINKING DEPT.

48

DEPT. OF RETRACTIONS

On May 7, 1983, President Reagan conducted a telephone interview with San Antonio radio station WOAI while aboard Air Force One. During the interview, Reagan was asked about Soviet leader Yuri Andropov's proposal to count nuclear warheads instead of missile launchers. Reagan said that "if it is a real offer, I could approve it." An aide then pointed out to him that his statement contradicted the policy of his arms control experts. As the plane was landing, Reagan told the interviewer, "I may have given people the wrong impression by using the word 'approved,' and what I should have said is we're looking seriously at this to see whether it's for real or whether ... it's just propaganda." (*Wash. Post*, 5/8/83)

Here we go again. Remember SALT II? Some people think those were real arms reduction talks, especially since that agreement called for significant reductions in arms between the superpowers. Remember Richard Nixon, Gerald Ford, Jimmy Carter? They all supported SALT II.

66 *When the United States was the only country in the world possessing these awesome weapons, we did not blackmail others with threats to use them.* 99 (3/31/83)

According to an analysis of this statement by the American Federation of Scientists, the US had an absolute nuclear weapons monopoly from 1945 until 1949, and an effective monopoly of long-range delivery systems until the early '60s. We "blackmailed others with threats" in August 1945 at Hiroshima and Nagasaki, Japan; in 1946 when Harry Truman suggested the USSR remove troops from Northern Iran; in November 1950, the day after marines were surrounded by Chinese troops at Chosen reservoir in Korea; in 1953 in an attempt by Eisenhower to get the Chinese into a settlement on Korea; in 1954 when John Foster Dulles asked the French if they'd like some awesome weapons to relieve the siege at Dien Bien Phu; in 1962, during the Cuban missile crisis.

66 *I have had some information in advance about it [the Catholic bishops' pastoral letter calling for a halt in the nuclear arms race] which indicates that it really is a legitimate effort to do exactly what we're doing. . . .* 99 (5/4/83)

Archbishop John R. Roach, president of the National Conference of Catholic Bishops, and Joseph Cardinal Bernardin, chairman of the committee drafting the bishops' letter, said they "could not accept any suggestion that there are relatively few and insignificant differences between US policies and the policies advocated in the pastoral."

GOOD-BYE, MR. KEYNES
Reagan & Economic Policy

Ronald Reagan's working model of the economy has one moving part—the free market mechanism. Strip away the heavy weight of taxes and government interference and you'll get a machine that works like crazy, churning out cars that people will always buy, steel mills that roar at full capacity, and trickle-down jobs for welfare mothers and black teenagers. But maybe the President should stop looking to the Gilded Age for inspiration. When Congress passed his tax and budget cuts nearly intact in the summer of 1981, he proclaimed that everything was in place for an economic renewal. The next month began not renewal but recession, the worst since the Great Depression. That takes some explaining. Instead we've been served up an unusually heavy dose of garbled statistics.

"... our state has been looted and drained of its financial resources in a manner unique in our history. ... For the last year the state has been spending $1 million a day more than it has been taking in. ... That means that by the beginning of the next fiscal year, we will have depleted our treasury by $365 million." (TV address, 1/30/67)

That June 30, the end of the fiscal year, a surplus appeared, right where Reagan said a deficit should be. In actual cash, it amounted to $9 million.

"In 1969, 100 new 'high risk' small business firms in such fields as electronics, energy research and development, and environmental management were incorporated. But that was 10 years ago. By 1976 there was not a single new small business formation in these fields." (Radio, Apr. 1979)

What Reagan is actually referring to is the clobbering the

DEPT. OF RETRACTIONS

In October 1982, Mr. Reagan told a state Republican party rally in Casper, Wyoming, that, "The truth is, thanks to your courage, your patience, and your support, we've already accomplished a minor miracle: we've pulled America back from the brink of [economic] disaster." Less than a month later the President seemed less sanguine. During a sound test for a radio speech, he said, "My fellow Americans, I've talked to you on a number of occasions about the economic problems and opportunities our nation faces. And I'm prepared to tell you, it's a hell of a mess." Reagan went on to ask, "We're not connected to the press now yet, are we?" He was. (*New York Times*, 11/21/82)

equity market received in the mid-'70s. It is true that new stock issues for venture capital in high technologies were zero in 1976, but that meant there were no public offerings of stock, not that there were no new businesses.

❝ I don't think the present [auto industry] crisis is due to the importation of foreign cars. I think it is due right now to the slump in the market because of 20% interest rates [since] most people buy automobiles on the installment plan. ❞ (Baltimore Sun, 4/30/80)

Reagan fails to explain in this analysis why purchasers of foreign cars don't face the same interest rates on car loans.

❝ . . . And they say the cost of food is responsible for X percent of the increase in inflation. That cannot be laid to the farmer. The farmer has actually been over the last 20 years reducing the percentage of family income that it takes to put food on the table. ❞ (New York Times, 5/1/80)

It is true that during the 1950s and '60s the percentage of the average family's income going for food dropped considerably, but that was not due to anything done by farmers. Food prices rose during that time, but incomes rose considerably more, thereby decreasing the percentage spent on food. Since 1970, that percentage has held steady at 18–20%.

❝ Their lives [the lives of workers and their families] have been shattered by a new depression—the Carter depression. The Carter depression was created and molded by Carter himself. ❞ (New York Times, 8/28/80)

Whatever Carter did mold it was not a depression, or at least not according to Reagan's own economic advisers. Alan Greenspan said, "I wouldn't have used that term." Martin

Anderson pointed out that most economists believed the nation to be in "a very severe recession." Anderson and his aides then went so far as to issue a clarification stating that "the Republican presidential nominee was not using the word 'depression' the way economists do." Oh.

❝ *One day, I publicly declared that this is a depression and the President before the day was out went to the press to say, 'That shows how little he knows. This is a recession.'* **❞** (*New York Times*, 10/19/80)

Not according to White House records or Reagan's staff. Said Reagan aide Lyn Nofziger: "I think it was Mondale who said that, and he didn't say it the same day. I think it was the day after, but it's good enough for us."

❝ *If America can increase its savings rate by just 2 percentage points, we can add nearly $60 billion a year to our capital pool to fight high interest rates, finance new investments, new mortgages, and new jobs. I believe a country that licked the Great Depression and turned the tide in World War II can increase its savings rate by 2 percentage points—and will.* **❞** (1/14/82)

◄ **WISHFUL THINKING DEPT.**

It may have been easier to win World War II. America has *never* increased its savings rate by 2 percentage points from one year to the next.

❝ *In the last 10 years, federal spending has increased more than 300%.* **❞** (3/15/82)

◄ **DIPSY DOODLE**

According to the 1983 budget of the United States government, federal spending (outlays) in current dollars increased by slightly more than 200% over the last 10 years. Adjusted for inflation—something Reagan always does when discussing

In a September 1982 speech before the Republican party faithful in Richmond, Virginia, the President explained, "Yes, America went backwards during those four Democratic years (1976–1980). The actual standard of living went down." Wrong again. According to Department of Commerce figures, per capita disposable income, the most precise economic measure of the standard of living, rose at an average annual rate of 1.8% during the Carter years, or nearly twice as fast as it has under Reagan in 1981–82.

the increase in military spending—federal spending has increased by 46.5%, not 300%.

❝ *Real earnings are at last increasing for the first time in quite a while.* ❞ (5/16/82)

Try decreasing. The Labor Department reported that in June 1982 real average weekly earnings for American workers declined 1.2%.

❝ *. . . I could point to comparisons that I've been drawing up of other democracies, allies, friends of ours like our own, who are continuing down the road of intervention in business—an adversary relation with their own business community—and the comparison I'm drawing is two sets of figures. Their unemployment is greater than ours, their inflation is greater than ours.* ❞ (9/28/82)

If only Reagan would go ahead with those comparisons, he'd get something more like the truth: that there's no clear link between government intervention and economic performance. Between 1970 and 1980, France's economy outperformed ours by around 41%—with a public sector some 27% larger. Germany, with one of the best inflation and employment rates for the '70s, had a public sector a third larger than America's. And Japan, with a smaller public sector than ours, somehow managed to have higher consumer inflation.

❝ *For four quarters we have seen a growth in the GNP.* ❞ (9/28/82)

Inflation-adjusted GNP had been declining for two of the four quarters under discussion.

SPECIAL REPORT #3

The Broken Record

Ronald Reagan based his viability as a candidate for chief executive on his performance as a two-term governor of California. The state of California, enjoying an economic boom, did not noticeably suffer during his eight years at the helm. But—and this is a big but—most of Reagan's oft-repeated campaign claims of tax-cutting, welfare reform, budget trimming, etc., are not substantiated by the facts. He bandied about a lot of numbers on the campaign trails of 1976 and 1980, numbers repeatedly disputed by California legislators, analysts, and journalists. But correction has never been enough to unstick the needle in the groove of Reagan misstatement. As president, he continues to cite as justification for current administration policy those same old non-accomplishments from the California record.

❝ *In California, with some realistic rules about determining eligibility, we reduced the [welfare] roles by more than 300,000 people in three years.* **❞** (*U.S. News & World Report,* 5/31/76)

The Welfare Reform Act of 1971 was Reagan's most heralded success. Campaign literature said it "best exemplifies his qualities as governor and as a leader." The precise number of reduced recipients claimed varies from 340,000 to 360,000. The Reform Act was responsible for only a small part of that reduction. The Institute of Business and Economic Research of the University of California at Berkeley concludes that the Act actually helped strike about 17,000 from the rolls. Outside factors must be given credit for the balance: the Therapeutic Abortion Act, which Reagan signed; a national trend toward smaller welfare families; a steadily improving (post-1970–71 recession) economy; and liberalized federal law. In fact, if you want to play a numbers game, just subtract the caseload low of 2,060,875 (from the January after Reagan left office) from

the caseload high of 2,292,945 (from six months before the reform became law) and you get a grand total caseload reduction of 232,070—only 2,070 more than the total number of Medicaid abortions in the same time period. Or, as state legislative analyst A. Alan Post put it, "The chiselers he is talking about are unborn children."

" *We reformed welfare in California and we saved $2 billion for the taxpayers over a three-year period. . . .* **"** *(Wash. Star, 3/2/80)*

There was never $2 billion to save. That figure represents money that would have been spent had the number of people receiving welfare continued to increase, even after the recession ended and the rate of abortion increased. Anthony Beilenson (D-Cal.) used these same calculations to figure out that by 1978 55% of the state's population would be on the dole; and that by 1984 everyone in the state of California, including the governor, would be on welfare. This claim sometimes appeared as "We *returned* $2 billion to the taxpayer," which is even more wrong.

" *We funneled 76,000 welfare recipients through that program [CWEP] into private enterprise and took them permanently off the welfare rolls. They're out there taking care of themselves now.* **"** *(Wash. Star, 3/2/80)*

The California Work Experience Program (CWEP) "put to work" only 4,760 welfare recipients—the figure of 76,000 refers to the number of people who left welfare to go to work regardless of whether the state helped them or not. A state legislative staff survey found that only 262 CWEP workers went into "private enterprise"—mostly as farm workers. This unimpressive performance led the state legislature to vote to abolish the program, a move Reagan vetoed in 1974.

" *. . . because I don't think government has a right to take one dollar more than government needs, we gave the surpluses back to the people in the form of tax rebates. We gave back over eight years $5.7 billion to the people of California. We stopped the bureaucracy dead in its tracks, the same way I would like to stop it at its national level.* **"** (*Wash. Post,* 4/27/80)

Reagan campaigned as "the greatest tax-cutter in the state's history" when, in fact, he was the greatest tax-hiker. The portion of the budget over which the governor has the most control—operations—increased under Reagan from $2.2 billion to $3.5 billion. State income tax revenues quadrupled, sales tax income tripled, and property tax revenue more than doubled. Reagan enacted the largest single tax hike in California history—a $1 billion omnibus tax rate increase. Tax brackets were narrowed in order to soak middle-class taxpayers. The top personal income tax went from 7% to 11%. The "rebates" consisted of shifting the incidence of taxation and redistributing revenues to local government—very little actually went back to taxpayers. As for the stopped-dead bureaucracy: the state budget more than doubled, going from $4.6 billion to $10.2 billion. One analyst put the eight-year increase in real terms as 85%. The number of state employees rose by 5.7% (in the same period, the number of federal civilian employees declined by more than 3%). In fact, the state coffers swelled with a surplus from all this increased taxation, a surplus that eventually spurred the populace into the tax-revolt known as Proposition 13.

" *Mr. Ford is overlooking a certain factor and that is that in 1966, I won the governorship in a state that is almost two-to-*

NEWS ITEM

The day he announced his candidacy for governor (1/4/66), Reagan claimed that "cracks have appeared in our economy," that the jobless rate in California was nearly 40% higher than in the rest of the country, and that California led the nation in bankruptcies and business failures.

The next day the Democratic Coordinating Committee set the record straight: California's 1965 economy was operating at far higher levels than any state in the nation; employment averaged 6,830,000, an all-time high; California simply did not lead the nation in bankruptcies. (*L.A. Times,* 1/5/66)

NEWS ITEM

In October 1973, Governor Reagan was vigorously promoting a referendum that would implement his planned reform of property and income taxes. He personally canvassed the state of California to drum up support. In the final days of this effort, a television reporter asked him, "Do you think the average voter really understands the language of this proposition?" Reagan replied, "No, he shouldn't try, I don't either." Proposition 1 lost three days later.

SPECIAL REPORT #3

one Democratic by a million votes and was re-elected by almost as many. 99 (*New York Times*, 3/3/80)

That "almost as many" was 497,000—otherwise known as half as many.

66 *And without exception in eight years, I took my appointments [to judgeships] from those who were rated [by review committees] as 'exceptionally well qualified.'* 99 (*New York Times*, 10/15/80)

Not quite. When the committees opposed his selection of aide William P. Clark, Jr., to California's highest court, Reagan made the appointment anyway. Clark is now President Reagan's National Security adviser.

TROJAN HORSES
Reagan & Taxes

Ronald Reagan pins the whole mess on Karl Marx. First, the bearded economist gave us Soviet Russia. Then, to put an extra nail in the coffin, he sent us the graduated income tax, and taxes are the number-one swindle in the eyes of the President. Why, he asks, do politicians think they can spend *our* money better than *we* can? Maybe the President has mixed up his centuries. In the old days monarchs did exact tribute, so they could build pyramids and castles, but nowadays the federal government spends *our* money on roads and schools. Conversely, a basic premise of Reaganomics is that sharply reduced taxes would make our economy walk again. But corporate taxes fell from 30% to 12% of all federal government revenues between 1950 and 1980, and we've been through several recessions in that time. Of course, this is merely fact. And since when did the President ever let facts get in the way of a good argument?

❝ *This whole progressive tax system is a* foreign import— *spawned by Karl Marx a century ago. He viewed it as one of the prime essentials of a socialist state. He said that in imposing socialism on a people, the progressive income tax should be used to 'tax the middle class out of existence.'* **❞** (*Screen Actor,* Sept. 1959)

Karl Marx is not the architect of our tax system, although in two lines in *The Communist Manifesto* he did say a graduated income tax would be an instrument of socialist policy.

The progressive income tax evolved gradually in the US from the income tax created during the Civil War. The 16th Amendment legalized the income tax, and the Act of 1913 provided its first progressive features. This legislation drew its inspiration from two economic philosophers, William Stanley Jevons (an Englishman) and Karl Menger (an Austrian).

◀ TALL TALE

Q: "Knowing of your great distaste for taxes and tax increases, can you assure the American people now that you'll flatly rule out any tax increase, revenue enhancers, or, specifically, an increase in the gas tax?"
A: "Unless there's a palace coup and I'm overtaken—or overthrown, no, I don't see the necessity for that." (9/28/82)

Q: "Mr. President, at your last news conference, you said it would take a palace coup for you to approve a $.05 a gallon increase in gasoline. . . . Have you changed your mind?"
A: "I don't think that I said it with reference to that. I said that on a general subject of tax increases, as such, it would take a palace coup." (11/11/82)

The President proposed the gas tax legislation to Congress on 11/30/82; he signed it into law on 1/6/83.

To them, the progressive income tax was the guarantee of a bourgeois society—it spread the tax burden equitably without destroying free market activity. The idea of the progressive tax as a bludgeon for the middle class was quite far from their minds.

❝ *What Congress, when they finished, gave him [Kennedy] was 30% [in tax cuts] at the bottom levels of the income earners and 23% at the top levels, and it averaged out to 27%. So . . . Kemp-Roth is asking for exactly what, in amount, Kennedy asked for.* ❞ (CBS Network News, 4/3/80)

Not exactly. In 1963, JFK requested a tax cut of 18%, weighted in favor of lower- and middle-income families. After his death, Congress enacted a 19% tax cut.

❝ *History shows that when the taxes of a nation approach about 20% of the people's income, there begins to be a lack of respect for government. . . . When it reaches 25% there comes an increase in lawlessness.* ❞ (*Time*, 4/14/80)

History shows no such thing. Income tax rates in Europe have traditionally been far higher than US rates, while European crime rates have been much lower.

❝ *The percentage of your earnings the federal government took in taxes in 1960 has almost doubled.* ❞ (2/5/81)

No. As a share of personal income, federal individual income taxes were 10.4% in 1960 and 12.0% in 1981.

❝ *The bipartisan [tax cut] proposal was designed to encourage small businesses. . . .* ❞ (7/27/81)

If so, the proposal was poorly designed. About 80% of the

Accelerated Cost Recovery System cut in corporate taxes were to go to the top one tenth of 1% of America's businesses, or those "small businesses" with assets of more than $250 million. Said William Hardman, a representative of the Small Business Legislative Council, "It would be difficult to write a tax bill better designed to speed the extinction of small business."

❝ *I mentioned the tax cuts in Coolidge's era. Every one of those tax cuts resulted in more revenues for the government because of the increased prosperity of the country as a whole.* **❞** (5/28/81)

TALL TALE

How about mentioning that in 1923, 1924, and 1927—when Coolidge was president—cuts in federal income tax rates led to a decrease in federal revenues. By 1929, the end of President Coolidge's terms in office, total Internal Revenue collections had dropped to $2.9 billion, down from $3.2 billion in 1922, the year before Coolidge took office.

❝ *Now, some of our business tax cuts are retroactive and go back to January 1, but, of course, they won't be felt until tax-paying time.* **❞** (*Wash. Post,* 10/1/81)

But, of course, some impact should already have been felt. Tax-paying time for businesses, as we hope the President is aware, comes every three months. According to the staff of the Congressional Joint Committee on Taxation, business tax breaks had already cost the government $1.6 billion in fiscal 1981.

❝ *As a matter of fact, if anyone wants to look closely, our original tax plan did not contain the reduction of the 70% bracket. That was suggested by the Democrats.* **❞** (11/12/81)

During the 1981 tax fight, Reagan displayed on television a numberless chart indicating a huge gap between the Reagan tax cut and the tax cut proposed by the Democrats. Actually, by 1986, a one-earner family would be paying $2,168 in taxes under his plan and $2,385 under the Democrats', a difference of only $217. Explaining the chart, Karna Small, deputy White House press secretary, said, "The President wanted to keep it as simple as possible."

No it wasn't. The original Reagan tax plan called for a lowering of the top rates from 70% to 50%, to be phased in over a period of three years. As David Stockman so memorably explained, "Kemp-Roth [the original GOP tax reduction proposal] was always a Trojan horse to bring down the top rate."

❝ *But I also happen to be someone who believes in tithing— the giving of a tenth [to charity].* ❞ (1/19/82)

He may believe, but he doesn't give. Larry Speakes informed the press the following day that the Reagans' total current charitable giving—$5,965 in cash contributions—did not approach 10% of total income. It was, in fact, more like 1.4%.

❝ *I would like to have them [the critics of his tax plan] give a specific on where this is a budget for the rich. The bulk of the personal income tax cut goes right across from the lower income to middle America.* ❞ (2/8/82)

Well, here are some specifics. According to the Congressional Budget Office, 35.1% of the tax cuts go to the wealthiest 5% of the taxpayers. The *National Journal,* using CBO and Census Bureau information, estimated that, had the 1983 tax cuts gone into effect in 1981, they would have taken $1.2 billion from the poorest fifth of the income spectrum and added $36 billion to the incomes of the richest fifth.

❝ *I would like to quote a few words by a very famous and celebrated orator, journalist, soldier, historian, and statesman. People have even said he might have made a great actor if he tried that. Winston Churchill. He said, 'The idea that a nation can tax itself into prosperity is one of the crudest delusions which has ever befuddled the human mind.' Now I don't know how that quote happened to catch my eye.* ❞ (3/9/82)

Neither does anyone else. Reagan's speechwriters "don't know where he got that one from." Nor does the British historian at the Library of Congress; there was no such passage in the Library's extensive collection of Churchill quotations. Ten other books of quotations also failed to provide a clue.

" *A tax shelter is only a shelter if you lose your investment. . . . And the fact is that, like so many others who have gone into government service, [William French Smith's tax shelter] was done by someone the Attorney General trusts to handle the investments he might have.* **"** (5/24/82)

A tax shelter permits you to take special tax writeoffs whether or not your investment earns a return. Reagan was also incorrect in blaming an investment counselor for the financial maneuver that converted a $16,500 investment into $66,000 in tax deductions—Smith's own office admitted two weeks before the President spoke that Smith "did it himself despite his blind trust that holds his assets."

" *Justice Oliver Wendell Holmes once said, 'Keep the government poor and remain free.'* **"** (6/15/82)

An official at the White House speechwriting office says the President "came up with that one himself. Holmes never said anything point-blank exactly like that . . . we're still trying to track it down." Professor Ed Bander of Suffolk Law School in Boston, a recognized Holmes scholar, didn't think Holmes "ever said anything that I can see which resembles that quote."

DEPT. OF RETRACTIONS

Speaking to the Massachusetts High Technology Council in Bedford, Massachusetts, the President surprised everybody when he asked, "But when are we all going to have the courage to point out that, in our tax structure, the corporate tax is very hard to justify. . . ." (1/26/83) Later that afternoon, a White House spokesman assured members of the press that "we're not seriously considering" repealing the corporate tax.

◄ **UNFAMILIAR QUOTATION**

Know Thine Own Ad Campaign

The following exchange, on the subject of the Reagan tax cut, took place on ABC's "Issues and Answers" between interviewers John Laurence and Bob Clark and candidate Reagan. The line of questioning quickly veered from the candidate's tax policy to the candidate's ability to remember his own television commercials. Lost in the shuffle was the fact that, even if he could remember what he was saying, it was incorrect—there never was a Kennedy "30% federal tax cut that became law." (Source: *The New Yorker*, 3/31/80)

JL: "You've been saying that you didn't always agree with President Kennedy, but that he found that a 30% tax cut helped almost everybody in the country, and if you were elected President you would cut taxes the same way he did."

RR: *"No, I didn't know what the rate of his tax cut was. I said that he went for a broad-based cut in the income tax. I don't know what the percent of that cut was but that it was contrary to all the economic advice being given and that it did result in an increase in revenues."*

JL: "If I can quote from your own ad, you're saying on camera 'I didn't always agree with President Kennedy, but when his 30% federal tax cut became law, the economy did so well that every group in the country came out ahead. If I become President, we're going to try that again.' Do you remember saying those words?"

RR: *"I don't remember saying that, because I honestly don't* know what the rate of the tax cut was."

JL: "Well, perhaps someone else wrote them for you?"

RR: *"I'm sure they did. But I don't even remember reading that."*

BC: "Coincidentally, I saw them in print this week, with your media adviser—fellow who puts together your media commercials—giving out the text, I believe."

JL: "Well, that raises the whole question of how familiar you are with the television ads that you do and . . ."

RR: *"Sure, I do them. I read them. And I suppose in the process of a whole afternoon, as you know, sitting in front of the camera and doing these things, and each one several times over, that I maybe just went by that one without thinking the 30% figure was familiar to me."*

Q: "Governor, did you pay any state income tax by the April 15 deadline?"

A (Obviously surprised): "You know something. I don't actually know whether I did or not."
(Press conference, 5/4/71)

He hadn't.

The Balancing Act

❝ *But I don't find any room for me in a debate on whether the deficit should be $52 billion or $70 or $80 billion. . . . That size deficit is extremely dangerous and will put us back on the inflationary spiral.* **❞** (Newsweek, 3/24/75)

❝ *We have no choice. This government must get back as quickly as possible to a balanced budget.* **❞** (New York Times, 11/21/75)

❝ *. . . I don't know whether it [a balanced budget] is political or not, but it is absolutely necessary.* **❞** (Wash. Post, 1/12/76)

❝ *Balancing the budget by cutting the cost of government is the Republican way.* **❞** (Wash. Star, 6/13/78)

❝ *With only a 2% reduction in spending, we would have a balanced federal budget.* **❞** (Savannah [Ga.] News, 3/2/80)

❝ *I believe the budget can be balanced by 1982 or 1983.* **❞** (9/21/80)

❝ *I have submitted an economic plan that I have worked out in concert with a number of fine economists in this country, all of whom approve it and believe . . . that it can provide for a balanced budget by 1983 if not earlier. . . .* **❞** (Presidential debate, 10/28/80)

❝ *I'm as committed today as on the first day I took office to balancing the budget.* **❞** (9/15/81)

❝ *This administration is committed to a balanced budget, and we will fight to the last blow to achieve it by 1984.* **❞** (9/21/81)

❝ *In the first place, I said that [a balanced budget] was our goal, not a promise.* **❞** (12/17/81)

THE BOTTOMLESS LINE
Reagan & the Deficit

It just keeps getting bigger. Reagan campaigned as a budget trimmer, but a look at his record as governor of California (see Special Report #3) shows that he hasn't always kept that promise in the past. John Anderson kept asking Reagan how he was going to cut taxes, increase defense spending, and balance the budget all at the same time. Now we know the answer. On taking office, Reagan declared with his customary certainty that "the only cause of inflation is all those federal deficits." Now we have lower inflation *and* higher deficits. Hmmm. The situation definitely calls for Ronald Reagan's special math. It's time to get on national television and shuffle some charts and diagrams around, throw out a bunch of numbers and percentages and comparisons—and hope that nobody in the home audience has the time to calculate whether any of the facts and figures are true. Meanwhile, the literal-minded among us are faced with an odd situation: The same president who supports a balanced budget amendment to the US Constitution heads the administration with the biggest federal budget deficits in American history. Hmmm.

❝ *Mr. Carter is acting as if he hasn't been in charge for the past three and a half years; as if someone else was responsible for the largest deficit in American history.* ❞ (Nationally televised campaign speech, 10/24/80)

Federal deficits totaled $195 billion under Mr. Carter. The latest budget projections suggest that during Mr. Reagan's four years the deficit will total nearly $800 billion.

❝ *Yes, there'll be a $45 billion deficit, but just think what that means. That means that that deficit would be double that without our program.* ❞ (3/3/81)

The 1982 budget deficit was more than double $45 billion *with* the President's program. At $110.6 billion, it was the largest deficit in history. Budget projections based on the Congressional Budget Office's data suggest that the cumulative deficit accrued during Reagan's four years will nearly equal the cumulative deficits accrued since the beginning of the Republic in 1789.

DIPSY DOODLE ➤

❝ *And already, we can tell you that that $90 billion deficit of 1983 will actually be smaller in proportion to the GNP than the deficits were in 1975–1978. . . .* ❞ (3/8/82)

Sounds good, doesn't it? Unfortunately, the 1984 budget of the US government estimates that the 1983 deficit will be 6.5% of GNP, which makes it larger, not smaller, than percentages of GNP for any single year between 1975 and 1978: 3.1% in 1975; 4.0% in 1976; 2.4% in 1977; 2.3% in 1978. In fact, when the House Budget Committee ranked post–World War II deficits as a percentage of GNP, Reagan's budgets for his term in office took four of the top five spots.

❝ *Our original [budget cuts] totaled $101 billion. . . . Our own representation from the Congress proposed compromising at $60 billion. Their counterparts from the Democratic side of the aisle proposed $35 billion.* ❞ (4/29/82)

House Budget Committee aides say that Reagan's $35 billion Democratic figure arbitrarily included only two categories of domestic spending: non-COLA (Cost of Living Adjusted) entitlements and non-defense discretionary appropriations. When other deficit-reducing methods are included—defense cuts, tax revenues, user fees—the Democrats' proposed deficit reduction is far greater than that proposed by the President or the Republicans. The Democrats' proposal would cut the deficit on average $135 billion a year for three years, while the Republicans would cut it by $121 billion, and Reagan by only $79 billion.

❝ We managed in less than one year to substantially slow the momentum of decades of growth in government. The new management of a failing company that made changes like this in only one year would soon be the talk of Wall Street. ❞ (5/4/82)

Any company that increased its deficit by some $200 billion in two years would soon be bankrupt.

◄ WISHFUL THINKING DEPT.

❝ The budget deficits, I don't think can be laid at any individual's door. We have—I could turn around and say how much less that deficit would be if the Democratic leadership that is now pointing this nice little thrust . . . if they had given us all that we asked for last year. . . . ❞ (Wash. Post, 7/29/82)

Earlier, before the deficits skyrocketed, Reagan thought they had given him all he asked for: "On behalf of the administration, let me say we embrace and fully support that bi-partisan substitute [Gramm-Latta Amendment]. It will achieve all the essential aims of controlling government spending, reducing the tax burden, building a national defense second to none, and stimulating growth and creating millions of new jobs." (4/28/81) And after the 1981 tax cut was passed, Reagan was asked, "Sir, have you now got your program in place? Ought it now to work the way you envision it?" Answered the President, "Yes." (7/29/81)

◄ DIPSY DOODLE

❝ A propaganda campaign would have you believe these deficits are caused by our so-called massive tax cut and defense buildup. Well, that's a real dipsy doodle, because even after our tax cuts are fully in place, they will barely neutralize the enormous Social Security tax increase approved in 1977. . . . Current and projected deficits result from sharp increases in non-defense spending. ❞ (11/16/82)

There he goes again. The 1981 tax cut will cut revenues by *$377 billion* over the 1982–85 period, while increased revenues from Social Security and Medicare taxes will be only *$78 billion*—the government loses *$299 billion*. Ignoring the effects of inflation, the only areas of growth aside from defense are interest on the debt, Social Security, Medicare, and other health and pension programs. In fact, according to a *Washington Post* analysis, if defense spending and taxes are kept at the levels proposed by the President, all federal programs except Social Security and other pensions, the court system, and a few other basic functions will have to be *terminated* in order to balance the budget by 1985.

WANT ADS
Reagan & Unemployment

Jobs, jobs, jobs. In 1980, Reagan was handing out promises to the unemployed like campaign bumper stickers. He just couldn't say often enough how badly he felt for the "common man" whose job was a casualty of the "Carter depression." Then he got elected. And one of the opening salvos of his administration was a bid to shorten the time covered by unemployment insurance—just as unemployment was increasing in volume and duration. As it reached double digits, Reagan unfurled want ads from the Sunday paper. The problem, he sought to explain, was not jobs, jobs, jobs, but able-bodied men (and he meant just men) willing to fill them. The plain truth is that since Reagan got *his* job, three million Americans have lost theirs.

❝ *We have reduced the number of employees by 2½% without a layoff or firing.* **❞** (Speech, Kansas State University, 10/26/67)

The California Mental Hygiene Department had laid off at least 200 people by July 1 of that year. The Department of Health had fired 250. That's 450 former state employees who would dispute the "without a layoff or firing" claim.

❝ *He [a Detroit steelworker] invited me to come to his back-yard for hot dogs, and he invited in some of his friends and neighbors, all of them unemployed automobile industry, steel, and construction workers.* **❞** (*New York Times*, 10/19/80)

The steelworker was invited to invite the candidate into his backyard by the candidate's public relations staff. Half of those present had jobs. During the campaign Reagan was often tempted to exaggerate the level of unemployment—about 7.5%

◀ TALL TALE

❝ *Unemployment insurance is a pre-paid vacation for freeload-ers.* **❞** (Sacramento *Bee*, 4/28/66)

66 *As far as I am concerned, the line between depression and recession cannot be measured in strict economists' terms but must be measured in human terms. When our working people—including those who are unemployed—must endure the worst misery since the 1930s, then I think we ought to recognize that they consider it a depression.* **99** *(Wash. Post, 8/26/80)*

WISHFUL THINKING DEPT. ➤

at the time of this statement. Since his election he seems better able to resist that particular temptation.

66 *If you'll remember, there were two million who lost their jobs in the last six months of 1980, during the election. . . .* **99** (1/8/82)

The number of people employed *increased* in the last six months of 1980, ending the year with 283,000 more people working than in July.

66 *I realize there's been an increase in unemployment. It's been a continuation of an increase that got underway in the last several months of 1980.* **99** (1/19/82)

Still wrong. In the last six months of 1980, unemployment declined from 7.8% to 7.3%. It declined further to 7.2% in July 1981, before beginning the climb to double-digit figures.

66 *There's a million more people working than there were in 1980.* **99** (1/19/82)

For the President to use absolute figures is misleading—the work force is always expanding, and so it is the *percentage* of unemployed people that is the critical figure. Anyway, he still got it wrong—according to the Bureau of Labor Statistics, there were only 27,000 more people employed in December 1981 than there were in December 1980.

66 *Well, one of the things that's needed was illustrated in the local paper on Sunday. I made it a point to count the number of pages of help-wanted ads in this time of great unemployment. There were 24 full pages of classified ads of employers looking for employees.* **99** (1/19/82)

This is not the first time that Reagan has pulled this "want ads" trick. After he alluded to 33½ pages of want ads in the Sunday *Washington Post* of March 15, 1981, the American Vocation Association analyzed the section. That organization found that nearly all of the 2,000 jobs listed required some kind of vocational training and approximately 85% required a high level of training. The association concluded that high unemployment rates and lots of want ads in Sunday papers only served to highlight the mismatch between current worker skills and marketplace needs.

❝ *We have, in some of the hardest-hit states, extended the unemployment insurance. There's nothing that strikes to my heart more than the unemployed. . . .* **❞** (3/31/82)

Then how come the Labor Department estimates that changes in the eligibility formula in the 1981 budget reduced extended benefits for 1.5 million jobless workers? Moreover, changes in the way a state becomes eligible for the extended benefit program had Michigan—the hardest hit of the states—thrown off that program for 13 weeks just prior to the President's heartfelt speech.

❝ *When . . . individuals charge [that] our administration fights inflation by putting people out of work, I say they're exploiting helpless people for political gain. It's the most cynical form of demagoguery.* **❞** (9/25/82)

Some of those "demagogues" are the President's top advisers: Treasury Secretary Donald Regan ("All I know is that our economy is slowing down and I think that's healthy, because we have to slow the economy down in order to get some of the inflation out of it"); Commerce Secretary Malcolm Baldridge ("A slight recession, I think, is almost necessary right now"); Council of Economic Advisers Chairman-designate

NEWS ITEM

In mid-April 1982, the President told a class of Illinois schoolchildren that unemployment had declined by 88,000 in March 1982. This contradicted the Bureau of Labor Statistics, whose figures showed that seasonally adjusted unemployment had *increased* in March by 279,000, to 9% of the work force. The White House explained that Reagan was referring to "raw" figures, before seasonal adjustments had been factored in by the Bureau.

◄ DIPSY DOODLE

❝ *Is it news that some fellow out in South Succotash someplace has just been laid off?* **❞** (3/16/82)

" If all of the unemployed today were in a single line allowing two feet for each of them, that line would reach from New York City to Los Angeles, California. All of this can be cured and all of it can be solved. " (Presidential debate, 10/28/80)

Martin Feldstein ("Extremists among both the supply-siders and monetarists who predicted that inflation would be reduced without raising unemployment have been decisively proven wrong"); presidential spokesman Larry Speakes ("[High unemployment] is the price you have to pay for bringing inflation down"); Office of Management and Budget Director David Stockman (high unemployment is "part of the cure, not the problem").

" I would also like to point out that there's a higher percentage of . . . employed today than has been true even in the past in times of full employment. " (9/28/82)

How about pointing out that the Bureau of Labor Statistics employment/population ratio, which measures the percentage of population over 16 years of age that is employed, was at 57% in September 1982 as against a high of 59.2% in 1979?

" We have been . . . increasing unemployment steadily . . . for probably a decade and a half. But it became very pronounced in the years between—well, from '77 through 1980 and then on into the depths of this recession. " (10/4/82)

Unemployment in 1975 was 8.5%; in 1980, it was 7.1%. It became "very pronounced" in 1982, when it averaged 9.7%.

" No, I want to be fair. Unemployment is 9.8%. When we took office it was 7.4%. Okay, I'll take blame for 2.4% of the unemployment. And if, as everybody is worried about, it goes to 10%, well then I'll take blame for 2.6%. " (10/6/82)

Let's be fair to everyone. In the past 30 years, here's how the unemployment rate changed during each president's term in office. Republicans: Ike, +3.7%; Nixon, +2.0%; Ford, +3.1%; Reagan, +2.4%. Democrats: JFK, −.9%; LBJ,

−2.3%; Carter, −.1%. It's hard to see why the Democrats should accept blame for 7.4% unemployment, when Republican presidents have always increased unemployment and Democratic presidents have always decreased it. Unemployment passed the 10% mark two days after the President's speech.

WISHFUL THINKING DEPT.

❝ But if a lot of businesses would take a look and see if they could hire just one person, it would be interesting to see how much we can reduce these unemployment rolls. . . . If everyone would just simply look at it from the standpoint there are more businesses in the United States than there are unemployed. ❞ (12/23/82)

Recalling Reagan's unemployment solution, a reporter covering the President's fly-in to Louisiana to inspect flood damage came up with this proposal: "If everyone on the trip would just take one bucket of water home and flush it down the toilet, we could solve the flooding problem."

TALL TALE

❝ I have a special reason for wanting to solve this [unemployment] problem in a lasting way. I was 21 and looking for work in 1932, one of the worst years of the Great Depression. ❞ (10/13/82)

According to *Reagan,* Lou Cannon's biography of Ronald Reagan, about two months after graduating from college the 21-year-old Reagan found work as a radio announcer, earning $100 a month. Soon after, his salary was raised to $300 a month, more than double the highest salary his father had ever earned.

AWFULLY LARGE OFFICES
Reagan & Big Government

A big fan of big government Ronald Reagan is not. "Get government off the back of business," he preaches. In this crusade, Washington, D.C., becomes a modern-day Babylon, crawling with regulatory sins and sinners. The deadliest sins: paperwork (all those government forms) and regulations (all those government rules). The most reprehensible sinners: EPA, OSHA, Highway Safety, FDA, and, in days of yore, HEW. "You don't have to spend much time in Washington to appreciate the prophetic vision of the man who designed all the streets going around in circles," Reagan quips. But then he didn't like Sacramento either. This loathing for government, this eagerness to prove that any program to aid the disadvantaged is nothing but a boondoggle and a money gobbler, leads him to contrive statistics and stories with unmatched vigor. The anti-government, anti-regulation, anti-Washington stance is the perfect vehicle for the righteous indignation Reagan is so good at. It is also the inspiration for some of his greatest gaffes.

66 *Fascism's private ownership, private enterprise, but [with] total government control and regulation. Well, isn't this the liberal philosophy?* 99
(*Newsweek*, 1/12/76)

66 *Today, no one denies the American people would resist the nationalization of industry. But in defiance of this attitude, the federal government owns and operates more than 19,000 businesses.* 99 (*L.A. Times*, 1/3/62)

If that number ever reached a thousand, Reagan would be lucky. The federal government has formed a number of corporations and enterprises—the Tennessee Valley Authority, the Saint Lawrence Seaway Corporation, the Export-Import Bank, the Government National Mortgage Association. No one knows for sure how many there really are; in its study of government enterprises and corporations, the National Academy of Public Administration never mentions more than a few hundred.

66 *It is estimated that small businessmen in America spend a*

total of 130 million man-hours a year filling out government required forms. **"** (Debate, 9/11/75)

In 1977, the Small Business Administration estimated that there were 5.978 million small businesses in America—making those back-breaking paperwork requirements an average of only 21.76 hours per business per year.

" *At one stage, some years ago, GE [General Electric] could produce light bulbs for half the price at which it was selling them and was in open competition with Sylvania and Westinghouse and all the others. But GE already had such a large share of the market that it didn't dare reduce the price as low as it could have, because if it captured any more of the market, it could have been in trouble with the government.* **"** (*Wash. Post*, 6/3/76)

GE spokesman William J. Barron: ". . . we are wholly unable to identify any single system . . . which had the effect of cutting in half the cost of manufacturing our household-type lamp bulbs."

" *I bet everyone in this room has, at one time or another, climbed a ladder. How we did it without their [OSHA's] 144 rules and regulations about ladder-climbing I'll never know.* **"** (*Sanford* [Me.] *Journal Tribune*, 2/10/78)

OSHA has two regulations on climbing ladders.

" *The Senate Energy and Natural Resources Committee has unanimously approved legislation which first confesses that in 1893 the US minister to the Kingdom of Hawaii did "unlawfully conspire" to overthrow the government of Queen Liliuokalani. It then goes on to set up an Aboriginal Hawaiian Claims Settlement Study commission. This commission will seek out*

NEWS ITEM

According to a February 26, 1966, story in the *Los Angeles Times*, Reagan, on his mismanagement-in-government high horse, asserted that as a result of state regulations, the California Board of Education would have to burn $180,000 worth of extra state-printed textbooks. Two days later State Board of Education president Thomas Braden pointed out that the textbooks in question would, on the contrary, *never* be burned. They would either be re-adopted, distributed as extra allotments, or donated overseas.

◀ **TALL TALE**

At a news conference in late May 1983, President Reagan pointed to Morris High School in the Bronx, New York, and the Johnston High School in Austin, Texas, as examples of what can be done to improve public education without federal intervention. But Morris High School principal Frances Vazquez says she hired 16 remedial reading teachers with funds from a Great Society Program. "If we didn't have these teachers it would be devastating," she adds. Adan C. Salgado, Johnston's principal, was also a little surprised by the President's comments. "He did not really understand our situation. He did not have all the facts."

No kidding. Reagan managed to ignore both a 1980 federal desegregation order and $3.4 million in emergency federal aid to the Austin district, both

descendants of the aboriginal Hawaiians and bestow on them a billion dollars. **"** (Radio, Feb. 1978)

Apparently a reference to legislation that, in December 1980, became Public Law #96-565. It authorizes the Native Hawaiians Study Commission to look into the needs of native Hawaiians and, by June 1983, write a report with recommendations to the Senate. The Commission is not authorized to bestow one red cent.

" *This one I'm sure will touch your heart. The health planners in Washington are determined to cut public health care costs by reducing 'unnecessary surgery.' According to them, that term fits such things as cataract operations and hysterectomies. However, if a man agrees to dress in women's clothes for a year the Public Health Service says Medicare should pay for his 'gender reassignment surgery.'* **"** (Radio, June 1978)

The health planners were suggesting that *some* of these oft-performed hysterectomy and cataract operations *might be* unnecessary and were therefore recommending a "second opinion" policy. As for transsexual surgery, the Public Health Service was not able to produce any evidence of an official recommendation; the Department of Health and Welfare, which oversees Medicare and Medicaid, considers such surgery "experimental" and thus not eligible for benefit coverage. An official at the Department did point out that as Medicare is for those 65 and over, the number of interested men would be minimal.

" *Do you remember that our government some time ago appropriated money to go into the automobile business—well at least for one car? The idea was that Washington could build a safe, non-polluting, economical, high-gas-mileage car to prove the automobile industry could (if they would) produce such cars* *using existing technology. Well, Secretary of Transportation Brock Adams has unveiled the Department's $250,000 ideal car. . . . According to the Secretary and Joan Claybrook, administrator of the National Highway Transportation Safety Agency, the government had proven that the automobile industry could achieve all of the federally mandated requirements if it really wanted to. Indeed, Ms. Claybrook made a speech to the Economics Club of Detroit claiming the $250,000 car could be produced at roughly present day production costs. But guess what? The magic car has never been tested to see if all those accolades and statistics are true. The California company that did the job for the government says there was no money in the budget for testing. The Secretary is blaming Ms. Claybrook and Ms. Claybrook's staff says she was not fully briefed and that her claims were—well—exaggerated.* **〞** (Radio, June 1978)

Reagan is referring to a $12 million program—which included money for testing—that aimed to produce cars, called research safety vehicles, in designs that would meet current Detroit production capabilities and 1985 federal highway safety standards. Several models were produced, one of them a redesigned 1977 Chevrolet intended to demonstrate that the era of the family car need not crumble in the face of safety and emission goals. The model was designed to meet certain specifications—just as cars in Detroit are—and was tested as it was being assembled—just as cars in Detroit are. At least 17 vehicles were assembled, not just one. In early summer 1978, members of Congress asked to see one of the cars, although final testing had not yet been done. This is where Reagan got the never-been-tested allegation. However, the car was subsequently tested and, as advertised, got 27½ miles per gallon, and crashed safely at 40 miles per hour. Another model, composed of several different Detroit-made cars, got 33 mpg, crashed safely at 50 mph, and met 1985

NEWS ITEM CONT.

of which Mr. Salgado considered crucial to the improved performance of his students. The President's willful misapprehension of the federal role in public education was too much for the *New York Times*, which found Reagan to be "as oblivious to contradiction and rebuttal as a tape cassette."

NEWS ITEM

Reagan said in Michigan that too much regulation was the "major reason" that Chrysler needed federal aid to avert bankruptcy. When asked to name some of these regulations, he responded: "Well, there are tens and tens of thousands of unnecessary regulations. I think that someone could list off some to begin with that have been mandated, but I don't think that would be the answer."
(*New York Times,* 5/16/80)

DIPSY DOODLE ➡

emission standards. The National Highway Traffic Safety Administration believed it had the potential for saving half of the gas used in 1978 and some 15,000 lives. Cars of that design were given to the French, German, and Japanese equivalents of Detroit, all of whom tested and found that it lived up to or exceeded claims. Needless to say, Mrs. Claybrook's staff never said either that she was not fully briefed or that the claims for the car were exaggerated.

❝ *It is reported that General Motors now has more than 20,000 full-time employees who don't help build automobiles. They just work on federal paperwork and regulations.* **❞** (Radio, Jan. 1979)

According to GM, about 5,000 employees—out of more than 500,000—are involved to some degree in government "paperwork," mostly on things like taxes. Reagan used this statistic constantly on the campaign trail in 1980. When told by interviewer Bill Plante that GM said it had 24,000 employees working on government-mandated programs, most of them as designers and engineers, and only 5,000 on forms, Reagan responded, "I should not have been saying it as I did and it disturbed me somewhat. I haven't heard any criticism of that one, but I thought, just doing paperwork it sounded like an awfully large office."

❝ *There has actually been an increase in the number of accidents under OSHA.* **❞** (*Wash. Post,* 1/25/80)

There's also been an increase in the total number of people at work—again, it's not absolute numbers but percentages that matter. And the number of deaths, injuries, and illnesses per 100 full-time workers declined from 10.9 in 1972, the first full year of OSHA's operation, to 8.7 in 1980.

> *When Chicago burned down they didn't declare it a disaster area. They just rebuilt it, the people of Chicago, and this is the kind of America we can have again.* (*Wash. Star*, 3/2/80)

This is the kind of America we've had all along: On October 10, 1871, the Secretary of War, General William W. Balknap, declared the Chicago fire "a national calamity." The mayor of Chicago gave absolute police authority to the US Army under Lieutenant General Philip H. Sheridan. Federal rations, tents, and other supplies arrived from all over the country. According to A. T. Andreas, author of *History of Chicago,* millions of dollars to aid the rebuilding of Chicago came from all over the US, from the federal government, and from several foreign governments as well.

> *The government allocates it [refined oil] and decides where it will go. . . . And that's why now, deeper in the south, in Florida right now and in California—believe it or not—the lines are beginning to form again in the gasoline stations. You know why? Because the federal agency . . . has forgotten that people in the south continue to drive as much in the winter as they do in the summer and the allocations are based on the idea that they would not drive as much based on the states in the northeast and the snow drifts and so forth that leave the car in the garage for a while.* (*Wash. Star*, 3/2/80)

A spokesman for the Department of Energy's Economic Regulatory Administration says no, gasoline allocation is not based on driving patterns of "states in the northeast." It is based on each state's drivers' use for the base year—summer and winter—of 1978.

> *What would I cut? . . . Right now the GAO has furnished the Congressional Budget Office with a list of 41 specific items.*

Q: "You are aware, I am sure, that the US has an utterly disgraceful number of murders. Do you believe that there's any correlation between the wide dissemination of guns in this country and this disgraceful record? And, in short, isn't it time for a truly effective gun control law?"
A: "We get back to the old argument again—and I have stated many times—you cannot find in the states, the various states that have gun control laws, that there is any proportionate difference in the crimes committed where there are those very strict laws and where they are far looser in their laws." (2/16/83)

Oh, yes you can. According to the 1981 FBI Uniform Crime Report, 63% of all homicides in the US are committed in the southern and western regions of the country, where handgun laws are the weakest.

NEWS ITEM

In Grand Island, Nebraska, Reagan asserted that one definition of the family then being used in Washington was "any two persons living together." Asked in Amarillo, Texas, to name the agency using that definition, he said that he did not know. No one else was able to come up with a government agency operating on such a definition, and none has stepped forward to claim the honor. (*New York Times,* 4/14/80)

FALSE ALARM ➤

All of them are totally unnecessary, spelled out right down to the penny . . . they total $11 billion [in savings], those 41 items. . . . **"** (*Wash. Star,* 3/2/80)

They totaled zero, those 41 items, at least as far as the Government Accounting and Congressional Budget offices are concerned—spokesmen for both said they knew of no such list.

" *There's a useless layer of bureaucracy up on top of HEW. And it costs HEW three dollars in overhead to deliver one dollar to a needy person in this country.* **"** (CBS Network News, 4/3/80)

It cost 12 cents to deliver one dollar of health care.

" *If you count the part of Alaska actually under the state's control, it's a smaller state than Rhode Island.* **"** (*New York Times,* 4/13/80)

A lot of Alaska *is* owned or controlled by the federal government, but not quite that much. Of Alaska's 586,412 square miles, about 80,000 are under state and private ownership. Rhode Island has 1,214 square miles all to itself.

" *If the figures that I've been given are correct, in these last three years the federal government has increased by 131,000 [workers].* **"** (*Time,* 4/14/80)

The figures were not correct. The Bureau of Labor Statistics put the average number of federal workers in 1976 at 2,733,000 and in 1979 at 2,773,000—for a grand total increase of 40,000.

" *Washington will be able to decide where you'll work, what kind of work you'll do, what you'll get paid, what you'll produce,* *and what the product will sell for.* **99** (*Wash. Post*, 4/23/80)

This description of the Humphrey-Hawkins Full Employment Bill is highly inflammatory. Neither the original legislation nor the compromise signed into law would do any such thing. The legislation prescribes the national goal of full employment, period.

66 *Up in Bellingham, Washington, HEW was threatening to take away the federal funds from the school district there, because they are spanking boys and girls in unequal numbers.* **99** (CBS Network News, 4/3/80)

Not quite. First of all, the school district was in Bellevue, not Bellingham. And the problem—at least as far as HEW was concerned—was discrimination against women in athletic facilities and vocational training. There did seem to be more cases of corporal punishment involving boys than girls, but HEW was not threatening to cut off funds for that reason.

66 *The government is actually making a sizable profit on that particular program [tobacco price supports].* **99** (*New York Times*, 5/1/80)

Reagan attempts to justify tobacco price supports despite his free-market philosophy. It doesn't work—according to tobacco specialists at the Department of Agriculture, the tobacco price supports cost the government in some years and make a little money in others, breaking even over the long run.

66 *Now last year [1979], the farmer's income—they talk about parity; I prefer to talk about net income, equity on their investment and on their equity—and actually their income pro-rated out to 90% of parity.* **99** (*New York Times*, 5/1/80)

66 *Property rights and freedom are inseparable. I believe that in a variety of ways, through environmental controls, through such things as OSHA, the government is trying to minimize the ownership of private property in this country.* **99** (*New Republic*, 5/24/80)

◄ LITTLE KNOWN FUN FACT

FALSE ALARM

Talking to corngrowers in Des Moines, Iowa, in August 1982, the President said that a congressman "from the heart of our biggest city" was once assigned to the House Agriculture Committee and promptly proposed "that government should confiscate all food and divide it equally among all the people because food was a natural resource belonging to everyone." According to the White House Press Office, however, "the story was not true; the President intended it as a joke."

LITTLE KNOWN FUN FACT ▶

Parity is an index that attempts to relate the purchasing power of farmers today to their power at the beginning of the century. According to the *Times*, "Parity can be measured in different ways, but by all measures it was far below 90% last year."

❝ [The Department of Education] is planning all manner of things to limit and restrict institutions of this kind [St. Joseph's College in Philadelphia] because their faith is totally in public education. ❞ (*The New Yorker*, 9/29/80)

No one in the press or Reagan entourage was able to come up with any idea of what the candidate might have been talking about.

❝ The federal government did not create the states, the states created the federal government. ❞ (Inaugural address, 1/20/81)

The original 13 colonies did get together and create our constitutional system, including the federal government. Yet the federal government "created" the other 37 states. Their land was either bought with federal monies or won at war by federal armies. Of the 37 states admitted to our nation after ratification, only Texas chose to become part of the US while a sovereign entity. The federal government did, however, assume Texas' debt when it became a state.

❝ In England, if a criminal with a gun, even if he was arrested for burglary, or theft, or whatever he was doing, was tried for first degree murder and hung if he was found guilty. ❞ (4/15/82)

A *New York Times* search of English law going back to the 14th century failed to turn up this legal standard. A member of the Law Society in Britain pointed out that there had once been a law that punished by execution the use of a gun that led to death, but never merely the carrying of a gun. After the error was pointed out, Press Secretary Larry Speakes commented, "Well, it's a good story though. It made the point, didn't it?"

66 *There is no relaxing of—in the field of antitrust or antimonopoly—on the part of our government at this time, nor will there be.* 99 (5/14/82)

Three months earlier the Reagan administration tried to eliminate antitrust enforcement by the Federal Trade Commission over the following three years by cutting off funding for the FTC's Bureau of Competition. Congress refused.

66 *[Alexis de Tocqueville said] 'You know, in America someone sees a problem that needs solving. And they cross the street and talk to a neighbor about it. And the first thing you know a committee is formed.' And he said, 'Finally, the problem is solved.' And he said, 'You won't believe this. But not a single bureaucrat had anything to do with it.'* 99 (11/12/82)

When asked if de Tocqueville really mentioned the word "bureaucrat," a White House spokeswoman said, "The President changed it a little." The more familiar quotation: "If a stoppage occurs in a thoroughfare, and the circulation of the public is hindered, the neighbors immediately constitute a deliberative body and this extemporaneous assembly gives rise to an executive power which remedies the inconvenience before anybody has thought of recurring to an authority superior to that of the persons immediately concerned."

HUH???

Q: "Don't you think that things might have been different if Hinckley hadn't had more difficulty in being able to get a gun?"

A: "Sure would have been more comfortable, except that at two o'clock in the afternoon, thereabouts, out there surrounded by many of you, he did what he did in an area that has about the strictest gun control laws that there are in the US." (2/16/83)

The only problem with the President's argument against strict gun control laws is that John Hinckley did not obtain his gun in strictly controlled Washington. Hinckley got his weapon at Rocky's Pawn Shop in Dallas, Texas, where all you have to do to get a gun is pay for it.

"UNKINDEST CUTS"
Reagan & Social Programs

When it comes to the circus act that is his economic program, Ronald Reagan is like the Flying Wallendas; he scorns the use of a safety net. Safety nets are for sissies, cheaters, and loafers—and if Reagan's taunting anecdotes over the years are any indication, that's exactly how he thinks of people on welfare. The poor exasperate Reagan for another reason; they aren't content with their lot. They should know they would be better off without those Great Society programs. And they should take it for granted that private charity will come to the rescue when the net is cut. They should, but for some reason they don't, and Reagan is hurt when people say he doesn't care about the poor; he was poor once himself, he says. But then, he was a Democrat once, too.

66 *We were told four years ago that 17 million people went to bed hungry every night. Well, that was probably true. They were all on a diet.* 99 (TV speech, 10/27/64)

66 *. . . . a faceless mass, waiting for hand-outs.* 99 (Description of Medicaid recipients, 1965)

66 *Today a newcomer to the state is automatically eligible for our many aid programs the moment he crosses the border.* 99 (Speech announcing candidacy, 1/3/66)

The truth of the matter was that immigrants to California had to wait five years before becoming eligible for benefits. Reagan acknowledged his error, but nine months later said exactly the same thing.

66 *Take the war on poverty—a matchless boondoggle, full of sound and fury, but still with no record of accomplishment to point to. . . . The latest is a multi-million-dollar scheme to set the Zuni Indians up in a cooperative store to retail their hand-craft jewelry. If it works (and the government says it will), they'll gross $150,000 a year. Overlooked is the pertinent fact the Zunis on their own are doing $2 million a year in the sale of their jewelry.* 99 (Speech before Merchants and Manufac-

turers Assoc., 5/16/66)

Quite distorted. The federal government did give the Pueblo Indians of Zuni, New Mexico, a grant, but it was for $208,741— hardly a multi-million-dollar figure. And the tribe asked for a delay in the expenditure of the funds until they could construct a new building themselves to house the cooperative. As to the $2 million their jewelry sales grossed, the Indians themselves received only a small fraction of it.

66 *There's a woman in Chicago. She has 80 names, 30 addresses, 12 Social Security cards, and is collecting veteran's benefits on 4 non-existing deceased husbands. And she's collecting Social Security on her cards. She's got Medicaid, is getting food stamps, and she is collecting welfare under each of her names. Her tax-free cash income alone is over $150,000.* 99 (New York Times, 2/15/76)

The "Chicago Welfare Queen" got a lot of play during the 1976 Republican primary. Sometimes she had 12 names and 30 Social Security numbers, sometimes she was also an unwed mother on AFDC. Candidate Reagan never bothered to point out to his shocked small-town audiences that his story was largely allegation and rumor. The woman in question, Linda Taylor, had been officially charged with using 4 aliases—not 80—and fraudulent collection of $8,000—not $150,000. She had not, at the time of Reagan's statements, been convicted of anything.

66 *If you are a slum dweller, you can get an apartment with 11-foot ceilings, with a 20-foot balcony, a swimming pool and gymnasium, laundry room and play room, and the rent begins at $113.20 and that includes utilities.* 99 (New York Times, 2/15/76)

NEWS ITEM

Concerned with the costs of California's medical care to the elderly, Governor Reagan announced in July 1967, "Something must be done before this ill-conceived program bankrupts the state."

Yet, even though Governor Reagan gave four choices for the size of the upcoming Medi-Cal deficit ($210 million, $71 million, $51 million, and $60 million), not one of them ever showed up on the state's balance sheet. By August, the projected deficit was dropped from California budget projections; state revenues had paid for all Medi-Cal costs— without cuts in benefits or participants.

The Governor did not own up to the fact that the predicted deficit had never appeared until January 1968. (L.A. Times, 1/11/68)

86

HUH???

One day in the 1980 campaign, Reagan visited the Santa Marta Hospital in a Chicano area of East Los Angeles. He told the institution's staff that he had asked a nun there whether the hospital got "compensation from Medicaid or anything like that." According to the candidate, she answered "no." "I appreciate your pride in that," he told the group.

A "puzzled senior administrator" later informed reporters that 95% of the patients at Santa Marta were subsidized by either Medicaid or Medicare. (*Time,* 10/20/80)

Reagan based this statement on a project in East Harlem called Taino Towers. At the time, the coordinating director of the project, Robert Nichol, pointed out the following: only 92 of 656 units had 11-foot ceilings, and only over the kitchen and living space to save what would otherwise be wasted corridor space; there was no way anyone could get such an apartment for $113.20—the going rate was more like $450 or a quarter of the family's income; the pool and gym and other facilities mentioned were shared with the 200,000 people who lived in the community.

❝ *For more than 20 years the federal government has been building low cost housing for the poor. And they're constantly passing new programs, as each one fails. To date, the score is they have destroyed 3½ houses for every one they have built.* **❞** (*New York Times,* 6/27/76)

A statement apparently based on a decade-old study, by Reagan's economic adviser-to-be Martin Anderson, of the first federal urban program. The ratio seemed plausible, according to the Ford administration, only if applied exclusively to tracts that urban renewal marked for slum clearance—frequently in order to make way for commercial, not residential, development.

❝ *In North Carolina, in Gaston County, I found that they gave $21,000 to the county to buy heating oil for people who were too poor to heat their homes. Now they've discovered that $20,500 of that went for administrators' salaries and expenses to supervise the buying of $500 worth of oil.* **❞** (*New York Times,* 6/27/76)

Not quite. For bookkeeping purposes, part of the county's anti-poverty staff was listed in the emergency heating program.

Wayne Daves, director of Gaston Community Action, says this maneuver allowed the county to qualify for an additional federal grant of $11,300 that was used exclusively for fuel.

❝ *I never suggested that Social Security should be voluntary.* **❞** (*New York Times*, 9/17/80)

Not never. Voluntary Social Security was a staple of Reagan's mashed potato circuit speeches of the '60s. For example: "Social Security ought to be voluntary . . . so those who can make better provision for themselves are allowed to do so" (*Human Events,* Nov. 1966). Or, "Don't exchange freedom for the soup kitchen of compulsory insurance" (*New York Times,* 1/17/76).

❝ *Now, again this statement that somehow I wanted to destroy it and I just changed my tune, that I am for voluntary Social Security, which would mean the ruin of it. Mr. President, the voluntary thing that I suggested many years ago was that with a young man orphaned and raised by an aunt who died, his aunt was ineligible for Social Security insurance because she was not his mother. And I suggested that if this is an insurance program, certainly the person who is paying in should be able to name his own beneficiary. That is the closest I have ever come to anything voluntary with Social Security.* **❞** (Presidential debate, 10/28/80)

He has come a lot closer than that. See above.

❝ *There has been a great deal of misinformation and for that matter pure demagoguery on the subject of Social Security. . . .* **❞** (Radio address, 9/24/81)

The misinformation is on the subject of just how much the President wants to cut. He has acted to eliminate Social Secu-

NEWS ITEM

The President told a Republican audience in December 1981 about a woman in Illinois who supported CETA budget cuts even though her own job would be eliminated. He added, "She is now employed in a $25,000-a-year job in the private sector. She says it beats daytime television."

But according to *New York Times* reporter Howell Raines, Sue Long, the woman in question, left her job to go on the Illinois *state* payroll, and never made the daytime television remark.

NEWS ITEM

To highlight a mid-March 1982 speech on abuses of federal funds, the President said that Stuart F. Kindrick, Jr., who suffered brain damage and partial paralysis as a result of an industrial accident in 1973, had lost his Social Security disability benefits because he had been improperly drawing them while holding a job for three years.

Later, however, Social Security officials said they had no proof Kindrick ever worked and drew payments simultaneously. Indeed, shortly before Reagan's accusation, Social Security officials decided Kindrick was too crippled to work and sent him $2,324 for the months his status had been in question. "If I'm working, I'd like to know where so I can go and pick up my check," Kindrick said, obviously disgusted by the whole affair. (*Chicago Sun-Times*, 3/24/82)

rity benefits for students who are children of deceased and disabled workers; proposed cutting the minimum benefit for Social Security recipients; and allowed his Health and Human Services Secretary to propose cutting benefits at 62 years of age—a proposal rejected by the Senate, 95–0.

❝ *Once we get the private sector in the driver's seat, we can go just as far as your imagination and inspiration can take us. For example: Pima County, Arizona, concerned about the impact of budget cuts, looked into their hot meals program for the elderly. They discovered that out of their $53,000 budget, $50,000 went for staffing and administrative overhead. So, they eliminated the overhead, ran the program with volunteers. They doubled the food budget to $6,000, saved $47,000, and ended up feeding twice as many people.* ❞ (1/14/82)

Reagan's imagination took him pretty far on this one. "There's nothing been saved in overhead," said Frances Freeman, director of the South Park Area Council in Pima County. She added that the President "got his figures a little mixed up." Last year the council spent "between $7,000 and $8,000" on food, not the $3,000 the President implied. People were working for the program as volunteers rather than on salary because federal grant money had run out—they were waiting for new funds before going back on the payroll. The increase in the number of people fed resulted from the closure of other government-sponsored facilities.

❝ *In 20 years, the federal budget increased five-fold and the cost of welfare grew ten-fold. But that didn't help many local governments which lost effective control of their communities. It didn't help small businesses hit by the highest interest rates in a hundred years. It didn't help the working poor and pensioners flattened by double-digit inflation and taxation.* ❞ (1/14/82)

It probably did. The standard of living has doubled since 1960. Accounting for inflation, per capita disposable income, the average income after taxes, rose, in 1972 dollars, from $2,709 in 1960 to $4,472 in 1980. In 1959, 22.4% of Americans lived below the poverty line. By 1981, that figure had been cut nearly in half.

66 *There has not been a cut in the overall spending on human resources.* 99 (1/19/82)

Yes there has. While the total budget the President submitted for 1983 is $32 billion bigger than the 1982 budget, defense spending alone is up $33.6 billion for 1983, and interest payments on the national debt are up another $13.4 billion. Despite Reagan's assertion, total spending for everything else—including "human resources"—will be down under the Reagan budget.

66 *I don't believe that there is going to be any cut that's going to affect students with true need. . . .* 99 (2/18/82)

In fact, the needier the student, the harder he or she would be hit by Reagan's student-aid cuts. For example, a college student whose family is unable to make any contribution currently relies on an aid package that includes a maximum Pell Grant, a Supplement Grant, a work-study job, a State Student-Incentive Grant, and a Direct Loan or Guaranteed Loan. President Reagan's proposed program would reduce that student's Pell Grant, take away the Supplemental Grant and the State Grant, reduce the work-study award by 28%, make Direct Loans scarcer, and make Guaranteed Loans more expensive.

66 *We haven't touched Social Security.* 99 (3/31/82)

TALL TALE

During the 1982 election campaigns, a Republican TV advertisement showed a white-haired mailman delivering July's Social Security check, which contained an automatic cost-of-living increase in benefits. "President Reagan kept his promise to the American people," the ad proclaimed.

In fact, Reagan *opposed* **the increase in Congress, which passed it anyway. Rep. Claude Pepper (D-Fla.), chairman of the House Committee on Aging, said that for Reagan to claim credit for the increase "lowers the art of deception to depths not explored since the Nixon administration."** (*New York Times,* 7/7/82)

WISHFUL THINKING DEPT.

When Reagan made this statement, Congress had already approved his proposal to eliminate Social Security benefits for students who were children of deceased or disabled workers, and to end the minimum benefit for future beneficiaries.

DIPSY DOODLE ➤

❝I hear the downbeat talk about . . . hunger and so forth. There'll be two times as many food stamps as there were in 1978. The increase is that much. ❞ (3/24/82)

The increase in *appropriations* is that much. But the price of food has increased 40% since 1978, and the average participation in the program has increased by 5.7 million people over the four-year period. According to the Congressional Budget Office, 5/6 of all households receiving food stamps will have their real benefits *reduced.*

TALL TALE ➤

❝A young man went into a grocery store and he had an orange in one hand and a bottle of vodka in the other, and he paid for the orange with food stamps and he took the change and paid for the vodka. That's what's wrong [with food stamps]. ❞ (*Chicago Sun-Times,* 3/26/82)

Let's get back to reality. According to Mary C. Jarratt, the assistant secretary of agriculture who oversees the food stamp program, change from food stamp transactions is limited to 99¢ in coin—hardly the price of vodka. Jarratt told a House nutrition subcommittee that such anecdotes, which she called examples in the extreme, "do not represent a constructive approach to the situation." She added, "We are following up on that with the White House . . . to find the source of the story."

❝About 3.4 million households will receive subsidized housing assistance at the beginning of 1983. By the end of 1985, under our proposals, 400,000 more households will be added to

the list. **" "** (3/29/82)

The President neglected to add that the increase of 400,000 households was 300,000 less than the 700,000 proposed under Carter. Congress, however, did not pass all the proposed Reagan cuts, so by 1985 there will be 4.1 million subsidized households.

" " *We have found in the first investigation that 57% of the stores that were investigated are selling items for food stamps that are banned. . . .* **" "** (*New York Times,* 4/1/82)

Quite misleading. The "investigation" was not based on a random sample. The USDA had "some reason to suspect a problem," according to USDA official John W. Bode, in all the stores investigated, which represented only 2% of the total number of stores in the program.

" " *. . . in an editorial in a paper this morning . . . they said we had less money for vaccinations for children and therefore there was going to be more sickness and perhaps more child death. Well, what they didn't see was that we actually have more money in for that program than we've had for others.* **" "** (*New York Times,* 4/1/82)

"They" didn't see it because the money wasn't there. In March 1981, Reagan proposed a $6 million reduction in the federal funds allotted to states for immunization. Six months later he requested an additional $2.2 million cut. Congress compromised on a $2.3 million cut—not an increase—in that program. With the cost of vaccines sharply on the rise, the number of children immunized will be sharply reduced—perhaps even cut in half by fiscal 1983.

" " *In the same editorial they criticized the women, infant and*

In a Saturday morning radio address in February 1983, Mr. Reagan had some harsh words for his critics, whom he described as "misery merchants" and "doom-and-gloom criers." To make everyone feel better, and prove just how wrong those critics were, he asserted that his administration was increasing spending in "the social safety net" by "almost one-fourth." This spending increase he characterized as "welfare, medical, nutrition, and housing assistance for our most needy citizens, plus compensation for the unemployed."

Try mostly compensation for the unemployed. Almost two-thirds of that reassuring increase in social spending was due to the rise in unemployment compensation costs resulting from the recession. As ever, actual spending for welfare and housing is

children nutrition program. And I'm sure at first glance they must have thought something had happened. It's been merged with another program and is in there at much greater money than it has ever had before. (*New York Times*, 4/1/82)

Something *had* happened—Reagan's budget proposed a $200 million cut in nutrition funds. Edwin L. Dale, Jr., Office of Management and Budget spokesman, said, "The President possibly misspoke slightly on that one."

There have only been smaller increases than some of our big spenders would have preferred. (5/8/82)

There have been no budget cuts. (6/15/82)

Wrong. Reagan's own budget shows a $3.805 billion cut in spending earmarked for training, employment, and labor services. Federal spending will also be lower—by $3.695 billion—in 1983 than in 1982 for three major programs that help the poor: Aid to Families with Dependent Children; Medicaid; and food and nutrition assistance, including food stamps.

The decrease in poverty I referred to earlier started in the 1950s. By the time the full weight of the Great Society programs was felt, economic progress for America's poor had come to a tragic halt. (9/19/82)

In 1967, the Field Foundation testified before Congress on hunger in America: "Wherever we went and wherever we looked, we saw children in significant numbers who were hungry and sick." A decade later, the Field team retraced its 1967 steps and found "far fewer grossly malnourished people in this country. . . ." They concluded that food stamps and other federal nutrition programs, implemented or inspired by

Great Society legislation, had made the difference.

66 The family at a poverty level, where they don't pay taxes, their income is more than $500 better off simply because of the decrease in inflation. 99 (10/6/82)

Or $600, $472, $400, depending on the President's mood. According to the Center on Budget and Policy Priorities, purchasing power for families at the poverty line has not gone up. When cuts in benefits that previously went to these families are included, many of the working poor have, more likely, lost ground.

66 The food stamp program alone had grown in 15 years from $65 million to $11.3 billion—an increase of more than 16,000%. 99 (10/28/82)

Boy, that is a big increase. But . . . in Fiscal Year 1966, over 2,700 counties, or nearly 90% of all counties in the United States, did *not* participate in the food stamp program. The program did not become nationwide until 1974. Comparing 1966 and 1981 expenditures is like comparing an embryo with a fully grown adult.

66 For example, you mention nutrition. Well, right now in our budget we will be providing for about a 12% increase in the people that are eligible for the nutritional programs over what they knew in 1980. 99 (2/16/83)

Right now that budget will be providing for 100,000 *fewer* recipients of WIC (Women, Infant and Children) nutrition aid in 1984 than it did in 1980, according to the Center for Budget and Policy Priorities.

66 Now, some people I've seen have suddenly seized upon a

NEWS ITEM CONT.

down since 1981, and will continue to go down under current administration proposals. In the same speech, the President quoted Abraham Lincoln: "Truth is generally the best vindication against slander." And so it is.
(*New York Times*, 2/16/83)

FALSE ALARM

DIPSY DOODLE

DIPSY DOODLE

figure that has to do with school lunches, and they've said, 'Ah, there's a reduction in the number of school lunches.' Yes, there is, because for one thing there's a reduction in the number of children in school. . . . Maybe the baby boom is over, but suddenly their enrollment has dropped. **99** (2/9/83)

The 1.5% drop in public school enrollment from 1981 to 1982 does not come close to accounting for the 12% reduction in the number of students in the school lunch program. Many schools were forced to drop out of the program in 1982 because federal reimbursement was drastically cut and the schools could not carry the cost. In all, more than 3 million children were cut from the federal school lunch program.

LITTLE KNOWN FUN FACT ➤

66 *There haven't been cutbacks in funding for public education.* **99** (5/23/83)

Reagan's own budget figures show there have been. Federal outlays declined by $.2 billion in fiscal 1982. There will be a further $.1 billion cut in fiscal 1983. When asked to justify the President's statement, a White House official said, "He doesn't believe there has been."

The Good Old Days

The Great Depression. Does Ronald Reagan have any idea what was really going on in this country in the 1930s? Riots, unrest, misery, discrimination, hopelessness—according to him, they never happened. FDR and the New Deal? Creeping fascism. Sure Reagan likes to quote Roosevelt—the man could make a speech—but that doesn't mean he likes FDR's ideas. Remember—while Reagan is piously invoking one of America's best-loved presidents, Reagan administration policy is steadily dismantling the programs FDR believed in.

❝ *Anyone who wants to take a look at the writings of the members of the brain trust of the New Deal will find that President Roosevelt's advisers admired the fascist system.* **❞** (*New York Times*, 8/17/80)

Some of the New Dealers made references to the efficiency of the Italian government. So did Winston Churchill. This does not add up to an admiration for fascism. Neither FDR nor the New Deal brain trust ever hinted at adopting that political program.

❝ *Many of the New Dealers actually espoused what has become an epithet—fascism. . . . Ickes, [Secretary of the Interior] Harold Ickes, in his book, said that what we were striving for was a kind of modified form of communism.* **❞** (*New York Times*, 12/23/81)

A White House spokeswoman said, "I don't know and can't find who he was referring to specifically." Arthur Schlesinger, Jr., who has read the Ickes diaries word for word, said there was nothing in them to substantiate such a charge.

❝ *Fascism was really the basis for the New Deal. It was Mussolini's success in Italy, with his government-directed economy, that led the early New Dealers to say, "But Mussolini keeps the trains running on time.* **❞** (*Time*, 5/17/76)

❝ *I've always thought my father, God rest his soul, had the common sense that he would know that temporary fixes wouldn't work.* **❞** (12/23/82)

Reagan made this comment in response to a reporter's question about what his own parents would have thought of a $5 billion public works program. The reason the reporter asked the question was that Reagan's father had been in charge of the WPA program in Dixon, Illinois. The President's answer directly contradicted his own 1965 autobiography, *Where's the Rest of Me?*: "There were no boondoggles in Dixon to speak of under the WPA; parks were created out of brush and swamp riverbeds, bridges over the river, and even a hangar at the new airport. Practically all the unemployed were able-bodied and capable, and they besieged him [Jack Reagan] for chances at working for their keep."

❝ *Roosevelt at one time made a statement that the federal government had to get out of the business of—we didn't call it 'welfare' then, we called it 'relief' . . . . As he explained, the federal government was not the proper agency for that.* **❞** (*New Republic*, 5/23/83)

After concluding that the federal government should "quit the business of relief," FDR, at the same time, went on to call for a federal program for those out of work that would replace relief with employment by means of the biggest peacetime appropriations ever.

❝ *I didn't desert my party. It deserted me. I looked up FDR's old platform, and I discovered that it called for a restoration of states' rights and a reduction in the national budget. . . . The Roosevelt that I voted for had promised to cut federal spending* *by 25%, had promised to return to the states and local communities authority and autonomy that had been unjustly seized by the federal government.* **"** (*The New Republic,* 5/23/83)

Roosevelt made the promise of slashing government spending and reducing federal influence in 1932. Reagan voted for FDR not only in 1932, but also in 1936, 1940, and 1944. "Indeed," said William E. Leuchtenburg, author of *In the Shadow of FDR: From Harry Truman to Ronald Reagan,* "Reagan's devotion to Roosevelt was greatest *after* he had put through the precedent-smashing legislation that centralized authority in Washington."

" *In the Great Depression, nothing like that [riots caused by economic hardship] ever took place when the situation was much worse. . . .* **"** (1/5/83)

Some incidents the President may have forgotten: Farmers in his native midwest sabotaged milk deliveries and food shipments, and stood by with shotguns to keep their homes from being foreclosed. Army troops brutally dispersed WW I veterans marching for a bonus in 1932. During the coal strikes in many states, police and sometimes state militia and the national guard arrested those "banding and confederating." Hundreds of mounted police stormed demonstrating auto workers in Detroit. Grocery stores in Oklahoma were raided during the food riots there. Ah, yes, those were the days.

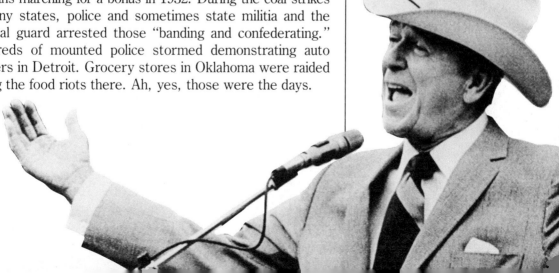

KILLER TREES
Reagan & the Environment

Look at it this way. If trees cause pollution, then what do we need a Clean Air Act for? We know where those killers are located, and so does James Watt. That must be why he's so eager to sell off sections of the National Park System to lumber companies—then you'd see those pollution indexes plummet. You may think this is a joke, but Ronald Reagan doesn't. He's out on the ramparts, beating back "snail darters" and other "extreme environmentalists" who won't be happy until the White House looks like a bird's nest. They're a wily lot, those environmentalists, forever trying to pin dead fish on big business. But it doesn't have to be this way. With the cooperation of the EPA (if only the US Congress would get out of its way) and the Department of the Interior (headed by James Watt, a man you can trust), Ronald Reagan is going to see that this country is made safe once again for the toxic-waste-dumping habits of huge corporations. As for an environment safe for the rest of us—well, don't hold your breath.

❝ *They [the federal government] are making it impossible for the people to have any access or enjoyment from [public] lands, unless, maybe, you're a backpacker who gets on them yourself.* ❞ (*Field & Stream,* 10/80)

❝ *Swarms of locusts and grasshoppers; a plague of crickets, cutworms, and ants; and swarms of mosquitoes are making life miserable and even impossible in some parts of the world. . . . Some experts are treating this as an unexplainable mystery. Actually, there is no mystery about it. . . . The most effective pesticide, DDT, was outlawed . . . on the theoretical grounds that it might, under some circumstances, some day, harm someone or something.* ❞ (Radio, Oct. 1978)

DDT's most prized characteristic, the ability to linger in the environment and to provide long-term effects, ultimately backfires, since insects develop resistance to it. Meanwhile, the rest of us are slowly poisoned as it builds up in the food chain. By 1972, DDT had been detected in 99% of human tissue samples taken in the US. It is a proven carcinogen. It has a devastating effect on birds, fish, and other wildlife. That's why the EPA banned its use in this country.

❝ *The world is experiencing a resurgence of deadly diseases spread by insects because pesticides such as DDT have been prematurely outlawed.* ❞ (*Chicago Tribune,* 5/10/80)

Nice try. Just because DDT's use is largely banned in this country doesn't mean it can't be manufactured here and sprayed elsewhere. In fact, the US exports more than 40 *million* pounds of DDT every year.

❝ *Approximately 80% of our air pollution stems from hydro-carbons released by vegetation, so let's not go overboard in setting and enforcing tough emission standards from man-made sources.* ❞ (*Sierra,* 9/10/80)

Talk about the commonsense gap. Trees do emit hydrocarbons, but the EPA does not find that cause for concern. Trees decay into nitrous oxide, which is not an immediate threat to human health. On the other hand, the EPA projects that emissions of man-made oxides of nitrogen—which are harmful and which those "tough emission standards are intended to control—will increase by 50% by the year 2000.

❝ *I know Teddy Kennedy had fun at the Democratic convention when he said that I had said that trees and vegetation cause 80% of the air pollution in this country. Well, he was a little wrong about what I said. First of all, I didn't say 80%, I said 92%, 93%, pardon me. And I didn't say air pollution, I said oxides of nitrogen. And I am right. Growing and decaying vegetation in this land are responsible for 93% of the oxides of nitrogen.* ❞ (*L.A. Times,* 10/9/80)

The gap becomes the Grand Canyon. According to Dr. Michael

◄ FALSE ALARM

◄ LITTLE KNOWN FUN FACT

WHAT A DIFFERENCE A DAY MAKES
4/17/67:
"I believe our country can and should have a Redwood National Park in California."

4/18/67:
". . . [T]here can be no proof given that a national park is necessary to preserve the redwoods. The state of California has already maintained a great conservation program."

"Air pollution has been substantially controlled." (Press release, 10/8/80)

"I don't think I've said anything of the kind." (Oct. 9, *Time*, 10/20/80)

"Isn't it substantially under control? I think it is." (*Time*, 10/20/80)

Oppenheimer of the Environmental Defense Fund, industrial sources are responsible for at least 65% and possibly as much as 90% of the oxides of nitrogen in the US.

“ *I have flown twice over Mt. St. Helens. I'm not a scientist and I don't know the figures, but I have a suspicion that one little mountain out there, in these last several months, has probably released more sulfur dioxide into the atmosphere than has been released in the last ten years of automobile driving or things of that kind.* **”** (*Time*, 10/20/80)

Not even close. Automobiles are not regulated for sulfur dioxide, since they emit very little of it—although, at 81,000 tons a day, they are still beating out the "little mountain" 's peak activity of 2,000 tons a day. Utilities, which *are* regulated for sulfur dioxide, have managed to generate 200 million tons of the stuff in the last decade, or 50 times the volcano's total output of 4,000,000 tons. No contest.

“ *As governor of California, I took charge of passing the strictest air pollution laws in the United States—the strictest air quality law that has ever been accepted.* **”** (Presidential debate, 10/28/80)

Dead wrong. It was under Governor Pat Brown, who preceded Reagan in office, that California adopted the toughest anti-pollution measures in the nation. Reagan did put his name to some air and water quality legislation, but only under the most intense pressure from California environmentalists. The record shows that during his eight-year reign as Governor, Reagan worked to undermine and weaken environmental standards. *California Journal* reported that by 1973 the Air Resources Board had "faded from national prominence into a strange kind of bureaucratic malaise, in which it inhibits rather than aids the smog-control effort." Shades of EPA present?

Why hasn't anyone mentioned that in response to that [a Sierra Club petition calling for the dismissal of Interior Secretary Watt], a petition of over seven million signatures was brought in wanting him retained? (1/21/82)

Probably because that petition never got seven million signatures. White House officials didn't know where Reagan got the figure, and Secretary Watt's office could only turn up a small article in the *Casper Star-Tribune* where Marlene Simons of Outdoors Unlimited—a national organization promoting multiple land use—reported the still-unbelievable sum of four million signatures. But Douglas Scott, who directed the Sierra Club's petition drive against Watt, says the Outdoors Unlimited petition claimed as signatures endorsements by organizations. For example, if the Farm Bureau endorsed the petition, they claimed the Bureau's entire membership as signatories. Scott estimated the real take as more like 100,000, while "nobody's in doubt about our 1.1 million signatures. Outdoors Unlimited cannot tell us where their petitions are."

The maintenance of a free, essentially self-governing scientific community is one of the great strengths of our nation. To undermine this tradition by requiring that the EPA Science Advisory Board wear the label "industry" or "labor" or "consumer" is a modern-day version of Lysenkoism to which I must strongly object. (Presidential veto, 10/22/82)

Webster's New World Dictionary defines Lysenkoism as "a repudiated doctrine that characteristics acquired through environmental changes can be transmitted by heredity." White House spokesmen were "not sure" what the President meant by the comparison.

Now there are 23 settlements [of hazardous waste dumping cases] so far that I know of. (2/16/83)

PROS & CONS:

REDWOODS

"A tree's a tree. How many more do you need to look at?" (Sacramento *Bee,* 3/12/66)

". . . 115,000 acres of trees in the state park system is a lot to look at. How long can you look?" (Sacramento *Bee,* 4/28/66)

"I'm a fellow who bleeds every time a tree is cut down." (Fresno *Bee,* 4/28/66)

"I don't believe a tree is a tree and if you've seen one you've seem them all." (Sacramento *Bee,* 9/14/66)

"I just didn't say it." (Associated Press, 10/5/66)

WISHFUL THINKING DEPT.

DEPT. OF RETRACTIONS

On November 30, 1982, President Reagan invoked executive privilege to prevent Congress from reviewing subpoenaed EPA documents. On February 16, 1983, the President apparently switched course. In a nationally televised news conference, he said that his administration "will never invoke executive privilege to cover up wrongdoing." He added, "I can no longer insist on executive privilege if there's a suspicion in the minds of the people that maybe it is being used to cover some wrongdoing."

The very next day presidential spokesman Larry Speakes insisted that Reagan had not said what everybody thought he had. Rather, the records would be submitted to the Justice Department, which would then decide whether it was "necessary" to hand them over to Congress.

That's 21 more settlements than the EPA knows of.

And so I have ordered a complete investigation by the Justice Department into every charge [of mismanagement and political manipulation of the Superfund at EPA] that is made. (2/16/83)

Not as far as Richard Hauser, a deputy to White House counsel Fred F. Fielding, was concerned. Asked by reporters about the President's statement, he admitted that the Justice Department investigation did not deal with mismanagement and that, if the political manipulation did not amount to criminal acts, "that would be the end of it as far as the Justice Department is concerned."

There is today in the United States as much forest as there was when Washington was at Valley Forge. (3/5/83)

Not even in the ball park, Mr. President—the amount of forest land in the United States has dropped significantly since George first wielded his ax. According to the US Forest Service, only about 30% of the 736.6 million acres of forest land that existed in 1775 still exists today.

I will match this administration's record with regard to environmental matters against that of any other administration. And we have been far more successful. We're spending more money on parks and on acquisition of parks and so forth than the previous administration had spent in all its four years, in these two years so far. (3/29/83)

Off by $1.4 billion. President Carter's four budgets for parks totaled $2.9 billion, according to Interior Department records. By the end of 1983, Reagan's budget will come to $1.5 billion.

SHORTAGE OF SENSE
Reagan & Energy Policy

Like an honest welfare recipient or a nuclear freeze movement free of Soviet agents, the idea of an energy shortage leaves Ronald Reagan baffled. After all, the President's America-first policy dictates a US reserve of oil larger than any other on earth. But that honor, despite our best efforts, stays with the Saudis. So maybe we could dismantle government regulation and the price system and still solve those energy problems. Problems such as aging transit and factory systems that waste fuel. Or oil prices that drop so much the oil men won't spend money finding hard-to-reach reserves. Or nuclear plants so costly and unreliable that the promise of abundant energy is the only thing cheap about them. The energy crisis, in short, is one of those national headaches with a long history and complicated origins. You could never tell that by the Reagan prescription: Take two aspirin, and leave on all the lights!

❝As for radiation, a coal-fired plant emits more radiation than a nuclear-powered plant. You even get more from watching TV or having your teeth X-rayed. ❞ (Radio, Nov. 1978)

False, according to Dr. Ernest Sternglass of the University of Pittsburgh. Coal-fired plants do not emit iodine or strontium-90 or cesium—dangerous sources of radioactivity that accumulate in vital organs such as the thyroid gland. Nor do TV sets or dental X-rays. Total radiation to organs is hundreds of times greater from a nuclear plant than from any of these sources. Moreover, federal law limits color TVs to emitting 0.05 millirems/hour at the screen itself—in other words, 1/10,000 of the federal radiation exposure limit (0.5 rems) for nuclear power plant operation.

❝It takes 12 years to get a nuclear power plant built in Amer-

"The truth is, all of the nuclear waste now on hand and yet to be accumulated between now and the year 2000, could be stacked on a single football field and the stack would only be six feet high." (Radio, Nov. 1978)

"The waste from one nuclear power plant in a year would take less storage space than a dining room table." (Radio, Apr. 1979)

"All the waste in a year from a nuclear power plant could be stored under a desk." (*Burlington* [Vt.] *Free Press,* 2/15/80)

These strange myths were exploded by Marvin Resnikoff in a July/August 1980 *Sierra* magazine article. The football field estimate is closest to reality— although only for a single plant's wastes for a single year of operation. The football field would also

ica. It only takes four or five in most other countries. The seven or eight years' difference is not construction time in our country; it is paperwork and the multitudinous permits required by the government. ❯❯ (Radio, Apr. 1979)

Wrong again. It does take ten to twelve years to build a nuclear power plant in the US, but that puts us ahead of India, Spain, Italy, and Britain, and behind Japan and France. In fact, the only country to do it in four years is Japan—once. As for the charge of regulatory sabotage, a congressional report concludes these claims "have been grossly exaggerated." The reasons for the French and Japanese lead are more logistical than bureaucratic. The Japanese work on their reactors around the clock, and the French have maximized efficiency by standardizing design.

❮❮ *Incidentally, the total radioactivity the people and the animals were exposed to in the immediate vicinity of the plant [Three Mile Island] was less than the difference between living in Dallas or living in the higher altitudes of Denver, Colorado.* ❯❯ (Radio, May 1979)

Reagan is again omitting the most important aspect of radiation, the internal dose to critical organs. This internal dose, which comes from breathing iodine in the air, drinking locally produced milk and the local water, etc., is about 100 times as much as the 70-millirem average difference between Dallas and Denver.

❮❮ *To put things in focus, Dr. Alvin Weinberg of Oak Ridge [National Laboratories] brought a Geiger counter to a committee room of the US Senate. It registered higher radiation than escaped at Three Mile Island.* ❯❯ (Radio, Aug. 1979)

Dr. Weinberg found the last sentence of the Reagan statement "difficult to interpret." He did in fact take a Geiger counter into a Senate committee room, and it did register five times the radioactivity that he had measured as "background" radiation at Atlanta Airport. While newspaper accounts of Three Mile Island radioactivity suggested that radiation levels were only two to three times "background," Weinberg believes that levels were probably much higher immediately after the accident. In any case, Weinberg's comparison applies only to gamma radiation and does not take into account the most dangerous forms of radioactivity—iodine, strontium-90, and cesium—which Senate committee walls do not emit.

66 *[Oil industry profits] were well below the average profit level of the rest of business and industry in America.* 99 (Ripon Forum, Oct. 1979)

Between 1974 and 1979, earnings per share for American oil and gas companies increased an average of 17.3%; for all industry the average increase was 12.6%. Other yardsticks of profitability—return on equity, return on total capital—put the oil industry either on a par with or slightly below, not well below, industry averages.

66 *What's wrong with adding a realistic energy policy in which we recognize the fact that right here in our own country we have the potential for the energy sources that we're presently importing?* 99 (*New York Times*, 1/2/80)

What's wrong is it's not realistic. Although American oil companies have stepped up drilling in the United States, they are beginning to wonder how sensible that policy is. Since the Prudhoe Bay discovery in the early '70s, no major tract of new oil wealth has been discovered in the US, and domestic reserves are steadily declining despite intense exploration.

TALL TALE CONT.

have to be underground, way underground. And it would not accommodate *all* the nuclear waste from the operation of a plant but only the *high-level* waste. A single nuclear plant's annual high-level waste might fit under your dining room table, but you wouldn't be able to go into the dining room—the waste would be generating too much heat and radioactivity. For those reasons, high-level waste has to be separated into small portions and spaced apart in a deep underground repository—no such repository has yet been sited or constructed. *All* the wastes from the nuclear energy process—including the remains from mining and milling uranium, low-level wastes from plant operation, the used plants themselves—would fill many, many football fields and still not be safely stored.

Whichever way you slice it, the US must continue to depend on the Arab states for much of its oil.

WISHFUL THINKING DEPT. ▶

We have more oil and gas yet to be found in America than we have used so far. (*New York Times,* 3/29/80)

Not really. The Department of Energy estimates that a total of 460 billion barrels of oil have been discovered in the US since 1867. Of that figure, 121 billion have been produced, and with today's technology we can get at 27 billion more. Recovery techniques still in the laboratory might be able to extract another 18–53 billion. That leaves 259 billion no one knows how to reach. As for natural gas—we've consumed about 650 trillion cubic feet since 1946. We have 201 trillion cubic feet to go.

Right now, we have seven plants, seven nuclear plants that are finished, completed . . . and yet they can't go on line producing electricity. They have not yet been able to get a license and the government go-ahead to do that. If they did go on line, instantly they would save us 700,000 barrels of oil a year. No, wait a minute, a day. (*Wash. Star,* 3/2/80)

Only four of the seven plants were ready for licensing at the time, according to the Atomic Energy Forum, the industry's leading trade association. Utility owners of six of these plants estimated that, together, they would stop buying a total of 100,000 barrels—not 700,000—a day. The owner of the seventh uses coal rather than oil to power his electrical system.

LITTLE KNOWN FUN FACT ▶

I've said it before and I'll say it again. The US Geological Survey has told me that the proven potential for oil in Alaska alone is greater than the proven reserves in Saudi Arabia. (*Detroit Free Press,* 3/23/80)

No matter how many times he's said it, it's wrong. According to the USGS, the Saudi reserves of 165.5 billion barrels are *17 times* the proven reserves—9.2 billion barrels—in Alaska.

"The windfall profits tax would cost one million barrels in the US a day in lost production in the first year." (*Time*, 4/14/80)

According to the US government estimate cited by *Time* magazine, the tax would cost 100,000 barrels a day, or a tenth of the Reagan estimate.

"Trains are not any more energy efficient than the average automobile, with both getting about 48 passenger miles to the gallon." (*Chicago Tribune*, 5/10/80)

The US Department of Transportation figures that a 14-car train traveling at 80 mph gets 400 passenger miles to the gallon. A 1980 auto with good mileage carrying an average of 2.2 people gets 42.6 passenger miles to the gallon.

"Nuclear power is the cleanest, the most efficient, and the most economical energy source, with no environmental problems." (*Sierra*, 9/10/80)

Cleanest? The entire nuclear fuel chain emits carcinogenic radiation, much more so than coal, although coal also is dirty. Wind and solar power are much cleaner, as is the most cost-effective "source" of energy, conservation.

Most efficient? The losses from electrical generation are large, since only a fraction of the thermal energy of a plant is converted into electricity, and more is lost in transmission. Natural gas, for example, is much more efficient.

Most economical? Nuclear costs more than coal, and much more than conservation, which can save a kilowatt-hour cheaper

"It would be wonderful eventually, but the technology is such that right now, to equal the power output we are getting from nuclear generators, we would have to cover the entire state of New York with mirrors. I don't think the environmentalists would hold still for that." (*Field & Stream*, Oct. 1980)

WISHFUL THINKING DEPT.

than it costs to make an additional kilowatt-hour.

No environmental problems? This is an incredible statement. There are problems with the disposal of radioactive mill tailings and radioactive waste. There are problems connected with continuous emissions of low levels of radiation. There are thermal pollution problems associated with warming bodies of water that are being used as plant coolant. And there is the "environmental" problem of nuclear war, which nuclear power makes more likely by making available necessary techniques, trained personnel, and fissionable materials to a number of countries that may not always have the best interests of the US uppermost in their minds.

DIPSY DOODLE ➤

❝ *Government regulations and production barriers are the two chief causes of the energy crisis we are in.* ❞ (*Science*, 10/10/80)

Try OPEC as a factor, and you get a clearer picture of the source of the energy crisis. In 1972, just before the first Arab oil emergency, the US devoted some 2% of its GNP to energy costs. In 1980, after the price of Saudi crude rose 750% in constant dollars, the country had to spend 8% of the GNP on energy. As for production barriers, when Congress dismantled most of them after 1973, the oil companies began to drill with a will, and oil and gas wells in Louisiana and along the Gulf began to dry up. Sometimes the oil isn't there even if you want it to be.

❝ *We have a profound responsibility that as we go forward with nuclear power, we must do it on the basis of every precaution for safety that can be taken.* ❞ (2/19/82)

While Reagan advocates caution, his administration throws it to the winds. For instance, there is a push to speed up licensing of nuclear power plants; the most dangerous aspects of

nuclear power are being promoted, including lifting Carter's ban on commercial reprocessing of spent fuel (despite lack of industry interest) and pushing the controversial breeder reactor; funds for alternative energy sources are being cut; delays are allowed in the implementation of safety procedures identified as a result of the Three Mile Island accident; backfitting of existing nuclear plants with new safety equipment is not being required of plants with relatively good records although their equipment is just as likely to wear out as plants that don't have good records; and finally, the administration proposes that the right of the public to participate in licensing be drastically curtailed.

T ERE OUGHTA N T BE A LAW
Reagan & Justice

What Ronald Reagan really doesn't like about our legal system is that, after many a fit and start, it often works the way it should. Blacks and whites protest against racial injustice; Congress and the courts, after much prodding, move to correct it. Legislators debate the legality of American aid to anti-Sandinista forces; the Boland Amendment defines what the government can and cannot do. Rules of evidence evolve to protect due process—but rarely prevent officers from making an arrest. Courts and Congress, lawyers and litigants, shake out the complex issues. Of course, Ronald Reagan and complexity go together like oil and vinegar. In *his* march of progress he'd much prefer a judicial lockstep, where presidential orations and Moral Majority invocations prevail: viz., the Supreme Court ban on school prayer is overturned; there is no affirmative action; former officials cannot publish uncensored memoirs; and the Legal Services Corporation stops operating. Ronald Reagan does want to guarantee our liberties, but he may not understand that he isn't the only one who gets to define them. Has he ever read the Freedom of Information Act? The Bill of Rights? The Constitution? Do you really want to know?

❝ *[The Rumford 'open housing' Act] was introduced into the Legislature in the last six minutes of the 1963 session . . . and was forced through hastily and without proper consideration.* **❞** (Speech, California Real Estate Assoc., 10/30/66)

The Rumford Act—designed to prevent discrimination in the sale of federally subsidized housing—was introduced early in the 1963 session, was the subject of extensive committee hearings, and was finally passed in the closing minutes of the session.

❝ *. . . first of all—the Hatch Act, there are some fifteen million* *public employees in the United States. If you grant each one of them only influence over one additional vote, such as a family member, you are talking about a voting bloc of 30 million people who conceivably can have any number of conflicts of interest. . . .* (NBC "Meet the Press," 5/1/77)

First of all, that voting bloc already exists. The Hatch Act, which prohibits federal employees from participating in political campaigns, does not prevent them from influencing the votes of their immediate family.

For many years the United Nations has had before it two covenants, the Covenant on Civil and Political Rights and the United Nations Covenant on Economic, Social, and Cultural Rights. Both specifically omit the right to own property or to be protected from arbitrary seizure without compensation. . . . What is apparently little known by the American people is that President Carter has signed both of these United Nations covenants which, in effect, nullify the inalienable right of an individual to own property—if they are ratified by the United States Senate, United Nations treaties become laws of the land, superceding all other laws. (Radio, Mar. 1978)

This is utter nonsense. Property rights are protected under the fourth, fifth, and fourteenth amendments to the US Constitution. A treaty or covenant that does not specifically take these rights away, as neither of these do, leaves those amendments fully in force. Besides, it is hardly logical that peanut baron Carter would have signed anything nullifying the right to own property.

[The United States Supreme Court is guilty of] an abuse of power as bad as the transgressions of Watergate and the bribery on Capitol Hill. (New York Times, 2/22/80)

PROS & CONS:

CIVIL RIGHTS ACT 10/19/65:
"I favor the Civil Rights Act of 1964 and it must be enforced at the point of a bayonet, if necessary." (L.A. Times, 10/20/65)

6/16/66:
"I would have voted against the Civil Rights Act of 1964." (L.A. Times, 6/17/66)

It doesn't do good to open doors for someone who doesn't have the price to get in. If he has the price, he may not need the laws. There is no law saying the Negro has to live in Harlem or Watts. (San Francisco Chronicle, 9/9/67)

The Court's "crime": to let federal abortion funding to poor women continue while it reviewed the power of Congress to cut off those funds.

[John Marshall] wasn't even a lawyer. (Presidential debate, 3/13/80)

The great Chief Justice of the US Supreme Court received his law license in 1780 and set up practice in 1783. According to Reagan aide Martin Anderson, Reagan meant to say that Marshall never went to law school, since his formal training was a matter of a few lectures at the College of William & Mary. Anderson: "He says it wrong. That's all."

TALL TALE

Mrs. Brown took this all the way to the Supreme Court because of her own memories of her childhood when she had to go miles past a school near her home simply because of segregation. And then she had a daughter of her own, and Mrs. Brown is opposed to busing in her own community because, she said, now her daughter is bused miles past the school near their home, and she said that wasn't what she had in mind. (10/4/82)

NEWS ITEM

In reply to a reporter's question at a Charlotte, N.C., news conference, Ronald Reagan said that the sit-in demonstrations waged by southern blacks in the '60s to gain access to public accommodations were wrong because they violated the law and the rights of others. (*New York Times,* 11/21/75)

Reagan's attempt to use Linda Brown Smith of *Brown* v. *Board of Education* to support his administration's anti-busing policy finds him once again at odds with reality. First, Linda Brown Smith's daughter recently graduated from the public high school two blocks from her home—Topeka doesn't bus children for racial balance. Second, Smith asked a federal judge to reopen her case because, she contended, her daughter was still the victim of *de facto* segregation in the Topeka school system. Third, Mrs. Smith's last public statement on the issue was pro-busing. On NBC's "Today," she told Phil Donahue, "I know what it is to have to get up early and go catch a bus in the cold and ride clear across town. But I also say if this is the solution, for now we should have busing."

66 *The First Amendment doesn't say anything about that [prayer in schools].* 99 (10/17/81)

It does, at least according to the Supreme Court of the United States. The Court ruled, in *Engle* v. *Vitale:* "Under that amendment's prohibition against governmental establishment of religion, as reinforced by the provisions of the 14th Amendment, government in this country, be it state or federal, is without power to prescribe by law any particular form of prayer which is to be used as an official prayer in carrying on any program of governmentally sponsored religious activity."

66 *If a policeman stops a car for a traffic violation and finds a sack of dope on the seat of the car, under the present case law, they can't introduce that—he can't arrest that man for a dope violation and use that dope as evidence because he stopped the man for a traffic violation.* 99 (1/27/82)

Certainly he can. As long as the policeman was stopping the car for a legitimate reason in the first place (a traffic violation is a legitimate reason) and as long as the sack of dope was "in plain view," the arrest is valid and the dope can be introduced as evidence.

66 *There's a law by which things of this kind [clandestine intelligence operations] have to be cleared with congressional committees before anything is done. . . .* 99 (2/18/82)

Not quite. The Intelligence Oversight Act of 1980 gives select intelligence committees of the Senate and the House the right to be *informed* of covert intelligence operations. They do not "clear" such operations—they have no veto power. The President may, in fact, delay notification—in some circum-

DEPT. OF RETRACTIONS

At a question and answer session with reporters, Reagan was asked whether he believed the *Weber* decision—which allowed firms to conduct voluntary affirmative action programs—should be overturned. He replied: "Well, if this [decision] is something that simply allows the training and the bringing up so there are more opportunities for them in voluntary agreement between the union and management, I can't see any fault with that. I'm for that." (12/17/81) Maybe he is, but his administration isn't. Assistant Attorney General William Bradford Reynolds has repeatedly emphasized that the administration's position is that it is illegal and unconstitutional to give preference to any group of people. The White House later retracted the President's remarks.

*❝ I am eternally opti-
mistic, and I happen to
believe that we've made
great progress from the
days when I was young
and this country didn't
even know it had a
racial problem. ❞* (Pres-
idential debate, 10/28/80)

DIPSY DOODLE ➞

stances—until the operation is completed.

*❝ The Constitution says . . . 'The right of the people to keep
and bear arms, shall not be infringed.' ❞* (Speech before
National Rifle Association, 5/16/82)

The full text of the Second Amendment reads: "A well regulated militia being necessary to the security of a free State,
the right of the people to keep and bear arms shall not be
infringed." The language Reagan omitted, the Supreme Court
has decreed, means that the military and the police can carry
arms, but that there is no constitutional right for citizens to
bear arms.

*❝ There are so few of those [finishing or preparatory] schools,
compared to the general parochial schools, throughout the country. But in this survey of 54 schools, they found 56% in those
parochial schools were black. ❞* (9/14/82)

Defending his plan to give tuition tax credits to families with
children in independent schools forces the President to over-
look the big picture. According to the US Census Bureau
(1975), there are 8.5 white families for every black family in
the US, and there are 17.8 white families with a child in a
non-public school for every black family. So a white child is
twice as likely to go to a non-public school as a black child.

*❝ The Justice Department has filed nine new anti-discrimi-
nation cases against public employers and has reviewed more
than 9,000 electoral changes to determine compliance with the
Voting Rights Act. And that, too, is a higher level of activity
than in any prior administration. ❞* (9/15/82)

The 9,000 reviews Reagan mentioned were those required
each time a state or local government covered by the Voting

Rights Act made a change in its election law, according to a report by the independent Washington Council of Lawyers. Such automatic reviews have been particularly numerous in the wake of the 1980 census that forced widespread redistricting. The Reagan administration filed only two new cases in the voting rights field during its first 20 months, compared to nearly a dozen in the first 12 months of the Carter administration.

66 *Sometimes, hearing that term 'the exclusionary rule'—this is a rule—it isn't a law; it's case law. It was a judicial decision once made that now has evidence thrown out of court even if they feel there was some technical violation in the way that the evidence was obtained. . . .* 99 (11/17/82)

Wriggle, wriggle. Reagan may not be crazy about the exclusionary rule, but that's no reason to pretend it's not law. The rule, which prohibits the use of evidence obtained in violation of the US Constitution, has been read by the Supreme Court from the 4th, 5th, and 6th amendments.

66 *The big spenders . . . even drove prayer out of the classrooms.* 99 (TV commercial, 10/31/82)

School prayer was abolished in 1962 by the Supreme Court's ruling in *Engle* v. *Vitale.* The Court does spend money on its operations, but it uses funds appropriated by Congress. When asked by the *New York Times* to identify the "big spenders," Mort Allin, an assistant White House press secretary, could not be specific. "They know who they are," he said.

NEWS ITEM

Upon signing an Executive Order reversing a 30-year trend toward less government secrecy, Reagan asserted that it would enhance "protection for national security information without permitting excessive classification of documents." Yet at a briefing for reporters following the signing, government officials acknowledged that *not one new provision* of the Order could be said to have been aimed at preventing overclassification or encouraging declassification of government records. (*Wash. Post,* 4/3/82)

Tax-Exempt Status

On January 8, 1982, the Reagan administration announced that it wanted to repeal a 12-year-old policy denying tax exemptions to private schools that discriminate on the basis of race. Critics howled. The *New York Times,* for example, asserted that the "Reagan administration is picking the pocket of every American taxpayer to subsidize racism in education." (1/19/82) As the story mushroomed, President Reagan used several rather large brushstrokes to paint himself into a corner as he attempted to explain why his administration did what it did.

1/12/82:

❝ *I am . . . opposed to administrative agencies exercising powers that the Constitution assigns to the Congress. Such agencies, no matter how well intentioned, cannot be allowed to govern by administrative fiat. That was the sole basis of the decision announced by the Treasury Department last Friday.* **❞**

The IRS was never acting by "administrative fiat." The Supreme Court in *Coit* v. *Green* (1971) explicitly concluded that the IRS *did* have a legal basis for its policy. And that policy was certainly not the IRS's own idea. When the case challenging the tax-exempt status of these schools came before the courts, the IRS fought it, maintaining that there was no constitutional obligation to use the tax laws to pursue school desegregation.

❝ *I didn't know there were any [segregated schools]. Maybe I should have, but I didn't. I was under the impression that the problem of segregated schools had been settled.* **❞** (Wash. Post, 5/12/82)

1/19/82:

❝ *What we were trying to correct was a procedure that we thought had no basis in law, that the IRS had actually formed a social law and was enforcing that social law. And we think that that's a bad precedent and is a bad thing to do, and so, there was no basis in the law for what they were doing.* **❞**

The law in the matter had been made clear by two Courts of Appeal and affirmed by the Supreme Court. For the past 12 years, the law has forbidden the IRS from giving tax-exempt "charity" status to discriminatory schools.

1/20/82:

66 I didn't know at the time [of the Executive Order] that there was a legal case pending. 99

Or so the President told William Raspberry of the *Washington Post.* The legal case Reagan was referring to was *Bob Jones University* v. *the United States,* which focused on the very issue of tax exempt status for segregated schools. However, according to a copy of a White House memo obtained by CBS News, the President *did* know of the case. The memo states that House Republican Whip Trent Lott (Miss.) "writes regarding pending cases concerning the tax exempt status of church schools. Indicates that the Supreme Court has now agreed to review case of *Bob Jones University* v. *the United States,* and urges you to intervene in that particular case." To the right of that summary, in the space reserved for comments, Reagan wrote: "I think we should."

1/21/82 (Wash. Post):

66 I'm the originator of the whole thing. 99

Fine.

President Reagan was originally opposed to the principle and substance of the 1981 extension of the Voting Rights Act: "I agree [that] . . . the perpetuation of punishment for sins that are no longer being committed is pretty extreme." (10/17/81)

Then this "extreme" bill passed the House and Senate by majorities of better than 10 to 1, was supported by Strom Thurmond, and was signed into law by the President himself. "Citizens," he said upon signing the bill, "must have complete confidence in the sanctity of their right to vote, and that's what this legislation is all about." (6/29/82)

THE REST OF HIM
Miscellaneous Distortions

Many of Ronald Reagan's distortions defy strict categorization. Over the years he has felt called upon to misstate the facts on a wide range of subjects. Sooner or later, it seems, he gets almost everything wrong. The result is a broad miscellany of error that proves an easily forgotten lesson: Ronald Reagan's grasp of detail is amazing. It's accuracy that gives him trouble.

FALSE ALARM ➤

In this week of tragedy, six policemen in Chicago have been killed in the line of duty. (*L.A. Times*, 6/14/68)

Respect for law and order had not sunk that year to the depths Reagan imagined. Chicago police records showed that only two officers had died on duty *since January 1, 1968,* one on June 5, and the other on May 4. The week of tragedy never existed.

[McGovern] did not become a peace advocate until . . . 1968 when he contracted Potomac fever. And he is still infected. (*L.A. Times*, 10/16/72)

McGovern first voiced opposition to Vietnam as a military boondoggle in 1963—that's five years before 1968. The day after he voted for the Tonkin Gulf resolution, he read into the congressional record his desire that no one construe his vote as support for growing involvement in Vietnam. On January 15, 1965—that's three years before 1968—he declared his opposition in a major speech. From that point on, he opposed every move to escalate bombing, increase troop strength, expand ground operations, etc.

NEWS ITEM

Governor Reagan's comment on the distribution of food in San Francisco demanded by Patty Hearst's kidnappers: "It's just too bad we can't have an epidemic of botulism." (*L.A. Times*, 3/7/74)

" To me, the simple argument is this: Is or is not the unborn child a human being? And from all that I learned in dealing with legislation on our state level, I am convinced that you are taking a human life when you interrupt a pregnancy. There's only one basis upon which we justify taking human life, and that's self-defense. " (US News & World Report, 5/31/76)

The legislation on the state level to which Ronald Reagan is referring was one of the most liberal abortion bills in the country. He signed it into law in 1967. And, it should be pointed out, every year thereafter, he also signed, without a peep, expenditure legislation targeting federal funds to finance abortions. Anthony C. Beilenson, who, as a state legislator authored the original measure, believes the liberal abortion law was one of the factors in the reduced size of welfare families—a big plus in Governor Reagan's highly touted crusade to trim the state's welfare rolls.

" Somehow they [young people] never seem to have heard the other side. Never heard, for example, that marijuana contains 300 or more chemicals and 60 of those are found in no other plant. " (Radio, Mar. 1979)

Before you get too excited, put this in perspective—tobacco smoke contains more than 3,000 chemicals.

" I had a great deal of sympathy [for blacklisted Hollywood actors], but I had just as much sympathy for the people whose careers were ruined by the Communists. They had a list, and if you were on their latest the phone stopped ringing and you didn't get called for parts anymore. They had more influence in the picture business than anyone has yet admitted. " (Christian Science Monitor, 5/14/79)

This interesting account of the period of blacklisting in Holly-

Q: "Governor, do you think homosexuals should be barred from public office in the United States?"

A: "Certainly they should be barred from the Department of Beaches and Parks." (L.A. Times, 12/5/67)

◄ **FALSE ALARM**

WHAT A DIFFERENCE A DAY MAKES

2/18/80:

"How do you tell who the Polish fellow is at a cockfight? He's the one with the duck. How do you tell who the Italian is at the cockfight? He's the one who bets on the duck. How do you know the Mafia was there? The duck wins." (*Wash. Star,* 2/18/80)

2/19/80:

"I don't like that type of humor, and in a conversation about stories once, this came about with one of the reporters on the plane and I had given this as an example. And on the bus, he [the reporter] asked me the other day, he said, 'What was the sequence of that story,' and I paused and told him, and . . . I think it's a cheap shot to use it." (*Wash. Post,* 2/19/80)

wood has never been corroborated. Countless books and articles have discussed the blacklisting *of* suspected Communists, but there seems to be woefully scarce examination of blacklisting *by* Communists. Frankly, it is hard to believe that the likes of Louis B. Mayer or Harry Cohn would have let lefties interfere in the operation of their studios, but you never can tell.

❝ *Shouldn't we ask if anyone has done a comparison of the situation before there was such education in the schools and after? I've had a report from one district that the venereal disease rate among young people in that district went up 800% in the first few years after sex education became a part of the curriculum.* ❞ (Radio, June 1979)

Since the school district is not named, it is difficult to track down the source of this report. However, a spokesman at the Atlanta Centers for Disease Control's VD division said they didn't know of any such circumstance and had not received such a report. He added that an 800% increase would be considered "a tremendous percentage rise in any communicable disease." Both Planned Parenthood of America and the Sex Information and Education Council said they "had never heard of such a thing." A spokeswoman at the American Social Health Association said that as far as she knew, no studies on a correlation between VD and sex ed had been done, and she had "no idea of what that figure is based on."

❝ *As president, I would be younger than all the heads of state I would have to deal with except Margaret Thatcher.* ❞ (*Wash. Star,* 11/12/79)

Reagan, who was 68 years old at the time, also made this assertion to Tom Brokaw on the "Today" show, who pointed out that Giscard d'Estaing of France would be younger. "Who?" responded Reagan. "Yes, possibly, not an awful lot more." Giscard d'Estaing was, at the time, 53. Chancellor Schmidt and Anwar Sadat were 60. Menachim Begin was 66. Lopez Portillo of Mexico was 59. Joe Clark of Canada, 40. And so on.

❝ *I have been told that some of the Iranians coming to this country are here to create disturbances and to form terrorist groups, and immigration officials know this because some of the things they found in their luggage, yet the State Department has said to the immigration people, 'Don't rock the boat.'* **❞** (*Time*, 4/1/80)

Reporters asked Reagan for corroborating evidence for this rather serious allegation—neither he nor his staff was able to provide any. It was not brought up again.

❝ *I am glad to be here where you're feeling it firsthand with the economic problems that have been committed, and he's [Carter's] opening his campaign down in the city that gave birth to and is the parent body of the Ku Klux Klan.* **❞** (*New York Times*, 9/2/80)

Aside from the question of taste in kicking off his drive for the presidency with a reference to the Klan, the facts are skewed. Carter was in Tuscumbia, Alabama. The Klan is traditionally thought to have been founded in 1866 in Pulaski, Tennessee.

❝ *President Carter has yet to be in one [debate], going clear back to when he ran for governor of Georgia and he reneged on a commitment to debate his opponent there.* **❞** (10/13/80)

Jimmy Carter debated President Gerald Ford three times in

HUH???

Q: "Governor, do you consider yourself born again?"

A: *"Well, I know what many of those who use that term mean by it. But in my own situation it was not in the religion, or the church that I was raised in, the Christian Church. But there you were baptized when you yourself decided that you were, as the Bible says, as the Bible puts it, that that is being born again. Within the context of the Bible, yes, by being baptized."* (*New York Times*, 5/27/80)

◄ LITTLE KNOWN FUN FACT

Elizabeth Drew wrote in the June 21, 1982 *New Yorker* of a White House meeting in which the President lauded the inventor of Rubik's Cube as exemplifying the virtues of American free enterprise. Erno Rubik, the inventor of the cube, is a Hungarian professor living in Communist Budapest.

TALL TALE ▶

the 1976 presidential campaign; the audiences averaged 60 million.

❝ *All we're doing is what every administration before us has done and we hadn't been doing.* ❞ (1/19/82)

Reagan made this statement in response to a question about a recently issued presidential directive that required administration officials to clear interviews with the press. According to Patricia Bario, deputy press secretary to President Carter, the Carter administration required "no preclearance at all." The Carter White House requested that officials notify it only after accepting a spot on a Sunday or morning TV show.

❝ *I think we're ahead of just about anyone at this point with regard to the appointment of women to high positions in our government.* ❞ (6/30/82)

Not ahead, not at that point. In the first 16 months of Carter's administration, he appointed 65 women out of 637 appointees to positions requiring Senate confirmation—or 10.2%. Under President Reagan, of the 679 people appointed to administrative positions requiring Senate confirmation, 51 were women—7.5%. And Sandra Day O'Connor notwithstanding, as of May 1982, the President had appointed only four women to 66 judicial positions—6%. By the end of his term, Carter had appointed women to 42 of 260 judicial openings—15.8%. A year after the President's statement, the US Civil Rights Commission said that it was "disappointed and concerned" about Reagan's record of appointing women and minorities to his administration, the federal judiciary, the US Attorney's Office, and the foreign service.

WISHFUL THINKING DEPT. ▶

❝ *David Stockman was betrayed by a longtime friend who*

distorted and misinterpreted things that had been said in complete confidence and the understanding that it was off the record. . . . 99 *(People, 12/27/82)*

David Stockman has never alleged that William Grieder, author of the December 1981 article in *The Atlantic* magazine called "The Education of David Stockman," violated his confidence. Grieder based his article on taped, on-the-record conversations with Stockman, who proved quite capable of betraying himself.

66 *It probably wasn't too much different from the press rushing into print with the Pentagon Papers, which were stolen—they were classified and it was against the law.* 99 *(6/28/83)*

"It" is completely different. This attempt by Reagan to wriggle out of the ethical problems raised by the alleged filching of Carter debate documents—"Debategate"—misfires. In *The New York Times Co.* v. *United States,* the Supreme Court ruled 6–3 that it was *not* "against the law" for the press to publish the Pentagon Papers. Nor has any court ever concluded the papers were "stolen." The criminal case against Daniel Ellsberg was thrown out of court. And in any event, it's hard to see how he could have stolen them since they were lawfully in his Pentagon office before publication.

NEWS ITEM

In April 1981, President Reagan pardoned two former FBI officials convicted of conspiracy for authorizing illegal break-ins of homes. "The record demonstrates that they acted not with criminal intent," he said, "but in the belief that they had grants of authority reaching to the highest levels of government." (*Newsweek,* 4/27/81) That's the exact opposite of the truth, for the jury specifically found that the two defendants *had* acted without the approval of higher-ups and in the full knowledge that such break-ins were unlawful. "We tried exactly that issue before the jury for eight weeks," said prosecuter John W. Nields, Jr.

People's Park

t was 1967. The Berkeley community felt that greed might have gone far enough. They wanted to keep an open plot of land near the campus undeveloped, the university wanted to put up another building. Violent confrontation ensued, with then-Governor Reagan typically using factual distortion to prove just how capricious, unwarranted, irresponsible, and invalid the student protest was. His comments are from a June 1967 speech.

" At no time did the squatters [on the university-owned lot] even designate an individual or a committee with whom the chancellor could communicate. "

Student body president Charles Palmer repeatedly contacted the chancellor to discuss the crisis, and on May 14, the People's Park advocates formed a committee to negotiate with the university.

" Now it has been learned that part of the lush greenery that was planted to make the lot a so-called sylvan glade turned out to be marijuana. "

Neither the police nor any other authority produced evidence that marijuana plants were growing in People's Park.

" There were no shortages of parks in Berkeley. "

There was no park at all serving the huge south campus area jammed with high-rise student residences and apartment buildings. The Berkeley City Council acknowledged the lack of open space and park facilities in the area.

❝ *The symptoms of student rebellion have been evident for some time. They no longer bother to vote in student elections.* **❞**

In a special referendum on the People's Park issue, more students (14,969) voted than in any election in the university's history. And 85% of them supported the "unauthorized" park.

NEWS ITEM

There are those who believe Reagan gaffes because he cannot hear. Sometimes the hearing problem is denied; sometimes, as during the 1980 campaign, it becomes another Reagan anecdote. According to the candidate, his hearing was affected years ago by an accident that occurred during filming, when another actor fired a gun so close to this head that "I staggered three or four feet" from the concussion. But, according to Dr. John Reynolds, Reagan's personal physician, the candidate does have a hearing loss in both ears that he described as "a normal consequence of aging." (*New York Times*, 6/11/80)

ADD YOUR OWN

"_____

_____

_____

_____

_____

_____ "

"_____

_____

_____

_____

_____

_____ " (   )

"_____

_____

_____ " (   )

"_____

_____

_____

_____ " (   )

"_____

_____

_____

_____

_____ " (   )

"_____

_____

_____ " (   )

"_____
_____
_____
_____" (   )

"_____
_____" (   )

"_____
_____
_____
_____" (   )

"_____
_____
_____
_____
_____" (   )

"_____
_____" (   )

"_____
_____
_____
_____" (   )

"_____
_____

"_____
_____
_____
_____
_____
_____
_____
_____"